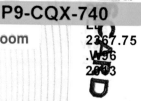
PRAXIS

SPECIAL EDUCATION: CORE KNOWLEDGE AND APPLICATIONS 0354

By: Sharon Wynne, M.S.

XAMonline, INC.
Boston

To obtain permission(s) to use the material from this work for any purpose including workshops or seminars, please submit a written request to:

XAMonline, Inc.
25 First Street, Suite 106
Cambridge, MA 02141
Toll Free 1-800-301-4647
Email: info@xamonline.com
Web: www.xamonline.com
Fax: 1-617-583-5552

Library of Congress Cataloging-in-Publication Data

Wynne, Sharon A.
    PRAXIS Special Education: Core Knowledge and Applications 0354 /
Sharon A. Wynne. 2nd ed
    ISBN 978-1-60787-347-1
    1. Special Education: Core Knowledge and Applications 0354
    2. Study Guides
    3. PRAXIS
    4. Teachers' Certification & Licensure
    5. Careers

Disclaimer:

The opinions expressed in this publication are the sole works of XAMonline and were created independently from the National Education Association, Educational Testing Service, or any State Department of Education, National Evaluation Systems or other testing affiliates.

Between the time of publication and printing, state specific standards as well as testing formats and Web site information may change and therefore would not be included in part or in whole within this product. Sample test questions are developed by XAMonline and reflect content similar to that on real tests; however, they are not former test questions. XAMonline assembles content that aligns with state standards but makes no claims nor guarantees teacher candidates a passing score. Numerical scores are determined by testing companies such as NES or ETS and then are compared with individual state standards. A passing score varies from state to state.

Printed in the United States of America   œ-1

PRAXIS Special Education: Core Knowledge and Applications 0354
ISBN: 978-1-60787-347-1

Table of Contents

DOMAIN III
INSTRUCTION

DOMAIN IV
ASSESSMENT

DOMAIN V
FOUNDATIONS AND PROFESSIONAL RESPONSIBILITIES

SAMPLE TEST

PRAXIS

PRAXIS SPECIAL EDUCATION: CORE KNOWLEDGE AND APPLICATIONS 0354

SECTION 1
ABOUT XAMONLINE

XAMonline—A Specialty Teacher Certification Company

Created in 1996, XAMonline was the first company to publish study guides for state-specific teacher certification examinations. Founder Sharon Wynne found it frustrating that materials were not available for teacher certification preparation and decided to create the first single, state-specific guide. XAMonline has grown into a company of over 1,800 contributors and writers and offers over 300 titles for the entire PRAXIS series and every state examination. No matter what state you plan on teaching in, XAMonline has a unique teacher certification study guide just for you.

XAMonline—Value and Innovation

We are committed to providing value and innovation. Our print-on-demand technology allows us to be the first in the market to reflect changes in test standards and user feedback as they occur. Our guides are written by experienced teachers who are experts in their fields. And our content reflects the highest standards of quality. Comprehensive practice tests with varied levels of rigor means that your study experience will closely match the actual in-test experience.

To date, XAMonline has helped nearly 600,000 teachers pass their certification or licensing exams. Our commitment to preparation exceeds simply providing the proper material for study—it extends to helping teachers **gain mastery** of the subject matter, giving them the **tools** to become the most effective classroom leaders possible, and ushering today's students toward a **successful future**.

SECTION 2
ABOUT THIS STUDY GUIDE

Purpose of This Guide

Is there a little voice inside of you saying, "Am I ready?" Our goal is to replace that little voice and remove all doubt with a new voice that says, "I AM READY. **Bring it on!**" by offering the highest quality of teacher certification study guides.

Organization of Content

You will see that while every test may start with overlapping general topics, each is very unique in the skills they wish to test. Only XAMonline presents custom content that analyzes deeper than a title, a subarea, or an objective. Only XAMonline presents content and sample test assessments along with **focus statements**, the deepest-level rationale and interpretation of the skills that are unique to the exam.

Title and field number of test

→Each exam has its own name and number. XAMonline's guides are written to give you the content you need to know for the specific exam you are taking. You can be confident when you buy our guide that it contains the information you need to study for the specific test you are taking.

Subareas

→These are the major content categories found on the exam. XAMonline's guides are written to cover all of the subareas found in the test frameworks developed for the exam.

Objectives

→These are standards that are unique to the exam and represent the main subcategories of the subareas/content categories. XAMonline's guides are written to address every specific objective required to pass the exam.

Focus statements

→These are examples and interpretations of the objectives. You find them in parenthesis directly following the objective. They provide detailed examples of the range, type, and level of content that appear on the test questions. **Only XAMonline's guides drill down to this level.**

How Do We Compare with Our Competitors?

XAMonline—drills down to the focus statement level.
CliffsNotes and REA—organized at the objective level
Kaplan—provides only links to content
MoMedia—content not specific to the state test

Each subarea is divided into manageable sections that cover the specific skill areas. Explanations are easy to understand and thorough. You'll find that every test answer contains a rejoinder so if you need a refresher or further review after taking the test, you'll know exactly to which section you must return.

How to Use This Book

Our informal polls show that most people begin studying up to eight weeks prior to the test date, so start early. Then ask yourself some questions: How much do you really know? Are you coming to the test straight from your teacher-education program or are you having to review subjects you haven't considered in ten years? Either way, take a **diagnostic or assessment test** first. Also, spend time on sample tests so that you become accustomed to the way the actual test will appear.

This guide comes with an online diagnostic test of 30 questions found online at *www.XAMonline.com*. It is a little boot camp to get you up for the task and reveal things about your compendium of knowledge in general. Although this guide is structured to follow the order of the test, you are not required to study in that order. By finding a time-management and study plan that fits your life you will be more effective. The results of your diagnostic or self-assessment test can be a guide for how to manage your time and point you toward an area that needs more attention.

After taking the diagnostic exam, fill out the **Personalized Study Plan** page at the beginning of each chapter. Review the competencies and skills covered in that chapter and check the boxes that apply to your study needs. If there are sections you already know you can skip, check the "skip it" box. Taking this step will give you a study plan for each chapter.

Week	Activity
8 weeks prior to test	Take a diagnostic test found at www.XAMonline.com
7 weeks prior to test	Build your Personalized Study Plan for each chapter. Check the "skip it" box for sections you feel you are already strong in. ✗ SKIP IT ☐
6-3 weeks prior to test	For each of these four weeks, choose a content area to study. You don't have to go in the order of the book. It may be that you start with the content that needs the most review. Alternately, you may want to ease yourself into plan by starting with the most familiar material.
2 weeks prior to test	Take the sample test, score it, and create a review plan for the final week before the test.
1 week prior to test	Following your plan (which will likely be aligned with the areas that need the most review) go back and study the sections that align with the questions you may have gotten wrong. Then go back and study the sections related to the questions you answered correctly. If need be, create flashcards and drill yourself on any area that you makes you anxious.

SECTION 3
ABOUT THE PRAXIS EXAMS

What Is PRAXIS?

PRAXIS II tests measure the knowledge of specific content areas in K-12 education. The test is a way of insuring that educators are prepared to not only teach in a particular subject area, but also have the necessary teaching skills to be effective. The Educational Testing Service administers the test in most states and has worked with the states to develop the material so that it is appropriate for state standards.

PRAXIS Points

1. The PRAXIS Series comprises more than 140 different tests in over 70 different subject areas.

2. Over 90% of the PRAXIS tests measure subject area knowledge.

3. The purpose of the test is to measure whether the teacher candidate possesses a sufficient level of knowledge and skills to perform job duties effectively and responsibly.

4. Your state sets the acceptable passing score.

5. Any candidate, whether from a traditional teaching-preparation path or an alternative route, can seek to enter the teaching profession by taking a PRAXIS test.

6. PRAXIS tests are updated regularly to ensure current content.

Often **your own state's requirements** determine whether or not you should take any particular test. The most reliable source of information regarding this is your state's Department of Education. This resource should have a complete list of testing centers and dates. Test dates vary by subject area and not all test dates necessarily include your particular test, so be sure to check carefully.

If you are in a teacher-education program, check with the Education Department or the Certification Officer for specific information for testing and testing timelines. The Certification Office should have most of the information you need.

If you choose an alternative route to certification you can either rely on our website at *www.XAMonline.com* or on the resources provided by an alternative certification program. Many states now have specific agencies devoted to alternative certification and there are some national organizations as well, for example:

National Association for Alternative Certification
http://www.alt-teachercert.org/index.asp

Interpreting Test Results

Contrary to what you may have heard, the results of a PRAXIS test are not based on time. More accurately, you will be scored on the raw number of points you earn in relation to the raw number of points available. Each question is worth one raw point. It is likely to your benefit to complete as many questions in the time allotted, but it will not necessarily work to your advantage if you hurry through the test.

Follow the guidelines provided by ETS for interpreting your score. The web site offers a sample test score sheet and clearly explains how the scores are scaled and what to expect if you have an essay portion on your test.

Scores are usually available by phone within a month of the test date and scores will be sent to your chosen institution(s) within six weeks. Additionally, ETS now makes online, downloadable reports available for 45 days from the reporting date.

It is **critical** that you be aware of your own state's passing score. Your raw score may qualify you to teach in some states, but not all. ETS administers the test and assigns a score, but the states make their own interpretations and, in some cases, consider combined scores if you are testing in more than one area.

What's on the Test?

The Praxis Special Education: Core Knowledge and Applications 0354 exam lasts 2 hours and consists of 120 multiple-choice questions. The breakdown of the questions is as follows:

Category	Approximate Number of Questions	Approximate Percentage of the Test
I: Development and Characteristics of Learners	19-20	16%
II: Planning and the Learning Environment	27-28	23%

Continued on next page

III: Instruction	27-28	23%
IV: Assessment	20-22	18%
V: Foundations and Professional Responsibilities	23-24	20%

Question Types

You're probably thinking, enough already, I want to study! Indulge us a little longer while we explain that there is actually more than one type of multiple-choice question. You can thank us later after you realize how well prepared you are for your exam.

1. **Complete the Statement.** The name says it all. In this question type you'll be asked to choose the correct completion of a given statement. For example:

> **The Dolch Basic Sight Words consist of a relatively short list of words that children should be able to:**
>
> A. Sound out
>
> B. Know the meaning of
>
> C. Recognize on sight
>
> D. Use in a sentence

The correct answer is C. In order to check your answer, test out the statement by adding the choices to the end of it.

2. **Which of the Following.** One way to test your answer choice for this type of question is to replace the phrase "which of the following" with your selection. Use this example:

> **Which of the following words is one of the twelve most frequently used in children's reading texts:**
>
> A. There
>
> B. This
>
> C. The
>
> D. An

Don't look! Test your answer. _____ is one of the twelve most frequently used in children's reading texts. Did you guess C? Then you guessed correctly.

3. Roman Numeral Choices. This question type is used when there is more than one possible correct answer. For example:

> **Which of the following two arguments accurately supports the use of cooperative learning as an effective method of instruction?**
> I.   Cooperative learning groups facilitate healthy competition between individuals in the group.
> II. Cooperative learning groups allow academic achievers to carry or cover for academic underachievers.
> III. Cooperative learning groups make each student in the group accountable for the success of the group.
> IV. Cooperative learning groups make it possible for students to reward other group members for achieving.
>
> A. I and II
> B. II and III
> C. I and III
> D. III and IV

Notice that the question states there are **two** possible answers. It's best to read all the possibilities first before looking at the answer choices. In this case, the correct answer is D.

4. Negative Questions. This type of question contains words such as "not," "least," and "except." Each correct answer will be the statement that does **not** fit the situation described in the question. Such as:

> **Multicultural education is not**
> A. An idea or concept
> B. A "tack-on" to the school curriculum
> C. An educational reform movement
> D. A process

Think to yourself that the statement could be anything but the correct answer. This question form is more open to interpretation than other types, so read carefully and don't forget that you're answering a negative statement.

5. **Questions that Include Graphs, Tables, or Reading Passages.** As always, read the question carefully. It likely asks for a very specific answer and not a broad interpretation of the visual. Here is a simple (though not statistically accurate) example of a graph question:

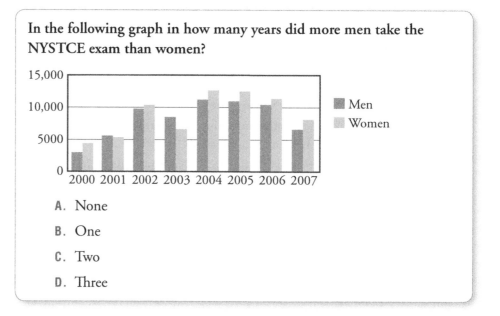

In the following graph in how many years did more men take the NYSTCE exam than women?

A. None

B. One

C. Two

D. Three

It may help you to simply circle the two years that answer the question. Make sure you've read the question thoroughly and once you've made your determination, double check your work. The correct answer is C.

SECTION 4
HELPFUL HINTS

Study Tips

1. **You are what you eat.** Certain foods aid the learning process by releasing natural memory enhancers called CCKs (cholecystokinin) composed of tryptophan, choline, and phenylalanine. All of these chemicals enhance the neurotransmitters associated with memory and certain foods release memory

enhancing chemicals. A light meal or snacks of one of the following foods fall into this category:

- Milk
- Rice
- Eggs
- Fish
- Nuts and seeds
- Oats
- Turkey

The better the connections, the more you comprehend!

2. See the forest for the trees. In other words, get the concept before you look at the details. One way to do this is to take notes as you read, paraphrasing or summarizing in your own words. Putting the concept in terms that are comfortable and familiar may increase retention.

3. Question authority. Ask why, why, why? Pull apart written material paragraph by paragraph and don't forget the captions under the illustrations. For example, if a heading reads *Stream Erosion* put it in the form of a question (Why do streams erode? What is stream erosion?) then find the answer within the material. If you train your mind to think in this manner you will learn more and prepare yourself for answering test questions.

4. Play mind games. Using your brain for reading or puzzles keeps it flexible. Even with a limited amount of time your brain can take in data (much like a computer) and store it for later use. In ten minutes you can: read two paragraphs (at least), quiz yourself with flash cards, or review notes. Even if you don't fully understand something on the first pass, your mind stores it for recall, which is why frequent reading or review increases chances of retention and comprehension.

5. Get pointed in the right direction. Use arrows to point to important passages or pieces of information. It's easier to read than a page full of yellow highlights. Highlighting can be used sparingly, but add an arrow to the margin to call attention to it.

6. Place yourself in exile and set the mood. Set aside a particular place and time to study that best suits your personal needs and biorhythms. If you're a night person, burn the midnight oil. If you're a morning person set yourself up with some coffee and get to it. Make your study time and place as free from distraction as possible and surround yourself with what you need, be it silence or music. Studies have shown that music can aid in concentration, absorption, and retrieval of information. Not all music, though. Classical music is said to work best

7. **The pen is mightier than the sword.** Learn to take great notes. A by-product of our modern culture is that we have grown accustomed to getting our information in short doses. We've subconsciously trained ourselves to assimilate information into neat little packages. Messy notes fragment the flow of information. Your notes can be much clearer with proper formatting. ***The Cornell Method*** is one such format. This method was popularized in *How to Study in College*, Ninth Edition, by Walter Pauk. You can benefit from the method without purchasing an additional book by simply looking up the method online. Below is a sample of how *The Cornell Method* can be adapted for use with this guide.

← $2\frac{1}{2}$" → Cue Column	← 6" → Note Taking Column
	1. Record: During your reading, use the note-taking column to record important points.
	2. Questions: As soon as you finish a section, formulate questions based on the notes in the right-hand column. Writing questions helps to clarify meanings, reveal relationships, establish community, and strengthen memory. Also, the writing of questions sets the state for exam study later.
	3. Recite: Cover the note-taking column with a sheet of paper. Then, looking at the questions or cue-words in the question and cue column only, say aloud, in your own words, the answers to the questions, facts, or ideas indicated by the cue words.
	4. Reflect: Reflect on the material by asking yourself questions.
	5. Review: Spend at least ten minutes every week reviewing all your previous notes. Doing so helps you retain ideas and topics for the exam.
↑ 2" ↓	**Summary** After reading, use this space to summarize the notes from each page.

*Adapted from How to Study in College, Ninth Edition, by Walter Pauk, ©2008 Wadsworth

8. **Check your budget.** You should at least review all the content material before your test, but allocate the most amount of time to the areas that need the most refreshing. It sounds obvious, but it's easy to forget. You can use the study rubric above to balance your study budget.

Testing Tips

The proctor will write the start time where it can be seen and then, later, provide the time remaining, typically fifteen minutes before the end of the test.

1. **Get smart, play dumb.** Sometimes a question is just a question. No one is out to trick you, so don't assume that the test writer is looking for something other than what was asked. Stick to the question as written and don't overanalyze.

2. **Do a double take.** Read test questions and answer choices at least twice because it's easy to miss something, to transpose a word or some letters. If you have no idea what the correct answer is, skip it and come back later if there's time. If you're still clueless, it's okay to guess. Remember, you're scored on the number of questions you answer correctly and you're not penalized for wrong answers. The worst case scenario is that you miss a point from a good guess.

3. **Turn it on its ear.** The syntax of a question can often provide a clue, so make things interesting and turn the question into a statement to see if it changes the meaning or relates better (or worse) to the answer choices.

4. **Get out your magnifying glass.** Look for hidden clues in the questions because it's difficult to write a multiple-choice question without giving away part of the answer in the options presented. In most questions you can readily eliminate one or two potential answers, increasing your chances of answering correctly to 50/50, which will help out if you've skipped a question and gone back to it (see tip #2).

5. **Call it intuition.** Often your first instinct is correct. If you've been studying the content you've likely absorbed something and have subconsciously retained the knowledge. On questions you're not sure about trust your instincts because a first impression is usually correct.

6. **Graffiti.** Sometimes it's a good idea to mark your answers directly on the test booklet and go back to fill in the optical scan sheet later. You don't get extra points for perfectly blackened ovals. If you choose to manage your test this way, be sure not to mismark your answers when you transcribe to the scan sheet.

7. **Become a clock-watcher.** You have a set amount of time to answer the questions. Don't get bogged down laboring over a question you're not sure about when there are ten others you could answer more readily. If you choose to follow the advice of tip #6, be sure you leave time near the end to go back and fill in the scan sheet.

Do the Drill

No matter how prepared you feel it's sometimes a good idea to apply Murphy's Law. So the following tips might seem silly, mundane, or obvious, but we're including them anyway.

1. **Remember, you are what you eat, so bring a snack.** Choose from the list of energizing foods that appear earlier in the introduction.

2. **You're not too sexy for your test.** Wear comfortable clothes. You'll be distracted if your belt is too tight or if you're too cold or too hot.

3. **Lie to yourself.** Even if you think you're a prompt person, pretend you're not and leave plenty of time to get to the testing center. Map it out ahead of time and do a dry run if you have to. There's no need to add road rage to your list of anxieties.

4. **Bring sharp number 2 pencils.** It may seem impossible to forget this need from your school days, but you might. And make sure the erasers are intact, too.

5. **No ticket, no test.** Bring your admission ticket as well as **two** forms of identification, including one with a picture and signature. You will not be admitted to the test without these things.

6. **You can't take it with you.** Leave any study aids, dictionaries, notebooks, computers, and the like at home. Certain tests **do** allow a scientific or four-function calculator, so check ahead of time to see if your test does.

7. **Prepare for the desert.** Any time spent on a bathroom break **cannot** be made up later, so use your judgment on the amount you eat or drink.

8. **Quiet, Please!** Keeping your own time is a good idea, but not with a timepiece that has a loud ticker. If you use a watch, take it off and place it nearby but not so that it distracts you. And **silence your cell phone**.

To the best of our ability, we have compiled the content you need to know in this book and in the accompanying online resources. The rest is up to you. You can use the study and testing tips or you can follow your own methods. Either way, you can be confident that there aren't any missing pieces of information and there shouldn't be any surprises in the content on the test.

If you have questions about test fees, registration, electronic testing, or other content verification issues please visit *www.ets.org*.

Good luck!

Sharon Wynne
Founder, XAMonline

DOMAIN I
DEVELOPMENT AND CHARACTERISTICS OF LEARNERS

PERSONALIZED STUDY PLAN

✘ **KNOWN MATERIAL/ SKIP IT**

PAGE	SKILL		KNOWN MATERIAL/ SKIP IT
3	1.1	Human development and behavior	☐
	1.2	Theoretical approaches to student learning and motivation	☐
	1.3	Basic characteristics and defining factors for each of the major disability categories	☐
	1.4	Impact of disabilities on individuals, families, and society across the life span	☐
	1.5	Impact of language, cultural, and gender differences on the identification process	☐
	1.6	Co-occurring conditions	☐
	1.7	How family systems contribute to the development of individuals with disabilities	☐
	1.8	Environmental and societal influences on student development and achievement	☐

SKILL 1.1 Human development and behavior

Children whose behavior deviates from society's standards for normal behavior for certain ages and stages of development are identified as having disabilities. Behavioral expectations vary from setting to setting; for example, yelling on the football field is acceptable, but yelling when the teacher is explaining a lesson to the class is not. Different cultures have different standards of behavior, further complicating the question of what constitutes a behavioral problem. People also have their personal opinions and standards for what is tolerable and what is not. Some behavioral problems are openly expressed; others are inwardly directed and not very obvious. As a result of these factors, the terms behavioral disorders and emotional disturbance have become almost interchangeable.

While almost all children at times exhibit behaviors that are aggressive, withdrawn, or otherwise inappropriate, the IDEA definition of serious emotional disturbance (SED) focuses on behaviors that persist over time, are intense, and impair a child's ability to function in society. The behaviors must not be caused by temporarily stressful situations or other factors such as depression over the death of a grandparent or anger over the parents' impending divorce. In order for a child to be considered seriously emotionally disturbed, he or she must exhibit one or more of the following characteristics over a long period of time and to a marked degree that adversely affects a child's educational performance.

- Inability to learn that cannot be explained by intellectual, sensory, or health factors

- Inability to maintain satisfactory interpersonal relationships

- Inappropriate types of behaviors

- General pervasive mood of unhappiness or depression

- Physical symptoms or fears associated with personal or school problems

Schizophrenic children are covered under this definition, and social maladjustment by itself does not satisfy this definition unless it is accompanied by one of the other conditions of SED.

The diagnostic categories and definitions used to classify mental disorders come from the American Psychiatric Association's publication Diagnostic and Statistical Manual of Mental Disorders (DSM-IV), the handbook used by psychiatrists and psychologists. The DSM-IV is a multiaxial classification system consisting of dimensions (axes) coded along with the psychiatric diagnosis. The axes are listed below.

> While almost all children at times exhibit behaviors that are aggressive, withdrawn, or otherwise inappropriate, the IDEA definition of serious emotional disturbance (SED) focuses on behaviors that persist over time, are intense, and impair a child's ability to function in society.

Axis I	Principal psychiatric diagnosis (e.g., overanxious disorder)
Axis II	Developmental problems (e.g., developmental reading disorder)
Axis III	Physical disorders (e.g., allergies)
Axis IV	Psychosocial stressors (e.g., divorce)
Axis V	Rating of the highest level of adaptive functioning (includes intellectual and social). Rating is called Global Assessment Functioning (GAF) score.

While the DSM-IV diagnosis is one way of diagnosing SED, there are other ways of classifying the various forms in which behavior disorders manifest themselves. The following tables summarize some of these classifications.

Externalizing Behaviors	Internalizing Behaviors
Aggressive behaviors expressed outwardly toward others	Withdrawing behaviors that are directed inward to oneself
Manifested as hyperactivity, persistent aggression, irritating behaviors that are impulsive and distractible	Social withdrawal
Examples: hitting, cursing, stealing, arson, cruelty to animals, hyperactivity	Depression, fears, phobias, elective mutism, withdrawal, anorexia, and bulimia

Well-known instruments used to assess children's behavior have their own categories and scales to classify behaviors. The following table illustrates the scales used in some of the widely used instruments.

Walker Problem Identification Checklist	Burks' Behavior Rating Scales (BBRS)	Devereux Behavior Rating Scale (Adolescent)	Revised Behavior Problem Checklist (Quay & Peterson)
Acting out	Excessive self-blame	Unethical behavior	*Major scales*
Withdrawal	Excessive anxiety	Defiant-resistive	Conduct Disorder
Distractibility	Excessive withdrawal	Domineering-sadistic	Socialized aggression
Disturbed peer relations	Excessive dependency	Heterosexual interest	Attention problems— immaturity

Continued on next page

Walker Problem Identification Checklist	Burks' Behavior Rating Scales (BBRS)	Devereux Behavior Rating Scale (Adolescent)	Revised Behavior Problem Checklist (Quay & Peterson)
Immaturity	Poor ego strength	Hyperactive expansive	Anxiety—withdrawal
	Poor physical strength	Poor emotional control	*Minor scales*
	Poor coordination	Need approval, dependency	Psychotic behavior
	Poor intellectuality	Emotional disturbance	Motor excess
	Poor academics	Physical inferiority—timidity	
	Poor attention	Schizoid withdrawal	
	Poor impulse control	Bizarre speech and cognition	
	Poor reality contact	Bizarre actions	
	Poor sense of identity		
	Excessive suffering		
	Poor anger control		
	Excessive sense of persecution		
	Excessive aggressiveness		
	Excessive resistance		

Disturbance may also be categorized in degrees: mild, moderate, or severe. The degree of disturbance will affect the type and degree of interventions and services required by the student with an emotional disturbance. Degree of disturbance also must be considered when determining the least restrictive environment and the services named for free, appropriate education for these students. An example of a set of criteria for determining the degree of disturbance is the one developed by P. L. Newcomer:

CRITERIA	DEGREE OF DISTURBANCE		
	MILD	**MODERATE**	**SEVERE**
Precipitating Events	Highly stressful	Moderately stressful	Not stressful
Destructiveness	Not destructive	Occasionally destructive	Usually destructive
Maturational Appropriateness	Behavior typical for age	Some behavior untypical for age	Behavior too young or too old
Personal Functioning	Cares for own needs	Usually cares for own needs	Unable to care for own needs
Social Functioning	Usually able to relate to others	Usually unable to relate to others	Unable to relate to others
Reality Index	Usually sees events as they are	Occasionally sees events as they are	Little contact with reality
Insight Index	Aware of behavior	Usually aware of behavior	Usually not aware of behavior
Conscious Control	Usually can control behavior	Occasionally can control behavior	Little control over behavior
Social Responsiveness	Usually acts appropriately	Occasionally acts appropriately	Rarely acts appropriately

Source: Understanding and Teaching Emotionally Disturbed Children and Adolescents, *(2ⁿᵈ ed., p. 139), by P. L. Newcomer, 1993, Austin, TX: Pro-De. Copyright 1993. Reprinted with permission.*

LANGUAGE: the means whereby people communicate their thoughts, make requests, and respond to others

COMMUNICATION COMPETENCE: the interaction of cognitive competence, social knowledge, and language competence

To effectively assess and plan for the developmental needs of individuals with disabilities, developmental areas of speech and language, fine and gross motor skills, cognitive abilities, emotional development, and social skills should be considered. In many cases, more than one area of development will be affected by a disability. In others, a problem that *can* be the result of a disability is actually the result of some normal factor in development. These things must be taken into consideration when interpreting a child's behavior and needs.

LANGUAGE is the means whereby people communicate their thoughts, make requests, and respond to others. **COMMUNICATION COMPETENCE** is an interaction of cognitive competence, social knowledge, and language competence. Communication problems can occur in any or all of these areas and have a direct impact on the student's ability to interact with others. Language consists of several components, each of which follows a sequence of development.

Brown and colleagues were the first to describe language as a function of developmental stages rather than age (Reid, 1988 p 44). They developed a formula to group the mean length of utterances (sentences) into stages. Counting the number of morphemes per one hundred utterances, one can calculate a mean length of utterance (MLU). Total number of morphemes / 100 = MLU, e.g., 180/100 = 1.8.

MLU AND LANGUAGE DEVELOPMENT		
Stage	MLU	Developmental Features
L	1.5–2.0	14 basic morphemes (e.g., in, on, articles, possessives)
LI	2.0–2.5	Beginning of pronoun use, auxiliary verbs
LII	2.5–3.0	Language forms approximate adult forms; beginning of questions and negative statements
IV	3.0–3.5	Use of complex (embedded) sentences
V	3.5–4.0	Use of compound sentences

Components of Language

Language learning is composed of five components: phonology, morphology, syntax, semantics, and pragmatics. Developmentally, children progress through each component.

Phonology

PHONOLOGY is the system of rules about sounds and sound combinations for a language. A phoneme is the smallest unit of sound that combines with other sounds to make words. Most phonemes have no meaning in isolation ("a" and "I" are exceptions). Generally, a phoneme must be combined with other phonemes to compose words or other morphemes. Problems in phonology may be manifested as developmental delays in acquiring consonants, reception problems such as misinterpreting words because a different consonant was substituted, or difficulty learning the sound-symbol code (phonics).

Morphology

MORPHEMES are the smallest units of language that convey meaning or function. **FREE MORPHEMES** are morphemes that can stand alone as root words, such as *walk* or *dog*. **BOUND MORPHEMES** are morphological units that do not stand alone. They convey or alter meaning when attached to other morphemes. Prefixes and

MORPHEMES: the smallest units of language that convey meaning or function

PHONOLOGY: the system of rules about sounds and sound combinations for a language

FREE MORPHEMES: units that can stand alone as root words, such as walk, or dog

BOUND MORPHEMES: morphological units that do not stand alone and convey or alter meaning when attached to other morphemes

MORPHOLOGY: the rules for making words, including rules for making plurals, possessives, and inflections in verbs

suffixes (e.g., pre-, -less), and inflectional endings (-ed, -ing) are examples of bound morphemes. MORPHOLOGY is composed of all the rules for making words, including rules for making plurals, possessives, and inflections in verbs. Content words carry the meaning in a sentence, and functional words join phrases and sentences. Generally, students with problems in this area may not use inflectional endings in their words, may not be consistent in their use of certain morphemes, or may be delayed in learning such morphemes as are used in irregular past tenses.

Syntax

SYNTAX RULES: govern how morphemes and words are correctly combined to make sentences

SYNTAX RULES, commonly known as grammar, govern how morphemes and words are correctly combined to make sentences. Wood, (1976, p.115) describes six stages of syntax acquisition.

- **Stages 1 and 2 (birth to about 2 years):** Child is learning the semantic system.

- **Stage 3 (ages 2 to 3 years):** Simple sentences contain subject and predicate.

- **Stage 4 (ages 2½ to 4 years):** Elements such as question words are added to basic sentences (e.g., where); word order is changed to ask questions. The child begins to use and combine simple sentences and to embed words within the basic sentence.

The child with a language disability manifests syntactic deficits by using sentences that lack length or complexity for a child that age. Such a child may have problems understanding or creating complex sentences and embedded sentences.

- **Stage 5 (about 3½ to 7 years):** The child uses complete sentences that include word classes of adult language. The child is becoming aware of appropriate semantic functions of words and differences within the same grammatical class.

- **Stage 6 (about 5 to 20 years):** The child begins to learn complex sentences and sentences that imply commands, requests, and promises.

Semantics

SEMANTICS: language content; the linguistic meaning of morphemes, words, phrases, and sentences

SEMANTICS is language content: the linguistic meaning of morphemes, words, phrases, and sentences. As with syntax, Wood (1976) outlines stages of semantic development:

- **Stage 1 (birth to about 2 years):** The child is learning meaning while learning his first words. Sentences are one word, but the meaning varies according to the context. Therefore, *doggie* may mean "This is my dog," "There is a dog," or "The dog is barking."

- **Stage 2 (about 2 to 8 years):** The child progresses to two-word sentences about concrete actions. As more words are learned, the child forms longer sentences. Until about age seven, items are defined in terms of visible actions. The child begins to respond to prompts (e.g., *pretty/flower*); at about age eight, the child can respond to a prompt with an opposite (e.g., *pretty/ugly*)

- **Stage 3 (begins at about age 8):** The child's word meanings relate directly to experiences, operations, and processes. Vocabulary is defined by the child's experiences, not the adult's. At about age twelve, the child begins to give dictionary definitions, and the semantic level approaches that of adults.

Semantic problems take the form of the following:

- Limited vocabulary

- Inability to understand figurative language or idioms; interprets literally

- Failure to perceive multiple meanings of words, changes in word meaning from changes in context, resulting in incomplete understanding of what is read

- Difficulty understanding linguistic concepts (e.g., before/after), verbal analogies, and such logical relationships as possessives, spatial, and temporal

- Misuse of transitional words such as *although*, *regardless*

Pragmatics

Commonly known as the speaker's intent, pragmatics are used to influence or control the actions or attitudes of others. **COMMUNICATIVE COMPETENCE** depends on how well one understands the rules of language and such social rules of communication as taking turns and using the correct tone of voice.

Pragmatic deficits are manifested by failures to respond properly to indirect requests after age eight (e.g., "Can't you turn down the TV?" elicits a response of "No" instead of "Yes" and the child turning down the volume). Children with these deficits have trouble reading cues that indicate the listener does not understand them. Whereas a person would usually notice this and adjust one's speech to the listener's needs, the child with pragmatic problems does not do this.

Pragmatic deficits are also characterized by inappropriate social behaviors such as interruptions or monopolizing conversations. Children may use immature speech and have trouble sticking to a topic. These problems can persist into adulthood, affecting academic, vocational, and social interactions.

Problems in language development often require long-term interventions and can persist into adulthood. Certain problems are associated with different grade levels.

Preschool and Kindergarten

The child's speech may sound immature. The child may not be able to follow simple directions and often cannot name such concepts as the days of the week

COMMUNICATIVE COMPETENCE: understanding the rules of language and such social rules of communication as taking turns and using the correct tone of voice

Pragmatic deficits are manifested by failures to respond properly to indirect requests. Pragmatic deficits are also characterized by inappropriate social behaviors such as interruptions or monopolizing conversations.

and colors. The child may not be able to discriminate between sounds and the letters associated with the sounds. The child might substitute sounds and have trouble responding accurately to certain types of questions. The child may play less with his peers or participate in nonplay or parallel play.

Elementary school

Problems with sound discrimination persist, and the child may have problems with temporal and spatial concepts such as before and after. As the child progresses through school, he or she may have problems making the transition from narrative to expository writing. Word retrieval problems may not be very evident because the child begins to devise strategies such as talking around the word he cannot remember or using fillers and descriptors. The child might speak more slowly, have problems sounding out words, and get confused with multiple-meaning words. Pragmatic problems such as failure to correctly interpret social cues and adjust to appropriate language, inability to predict consequences, and inability to formulate requests to obtain new information show up in social situations.

Secondary school

At this level, difficulties become more subtle. The child cannot use and understand higher-level syntax, semantics, and pragmatics. If the child has problems with auditory language, he may also have problems with short-term memory. Receptive and expressive language delays impair the child's ability to learn effectively. The child often cannot organize and categorize the information received in school. Problems associated with pragmatic deficiencies persist but, because the child is aware of them, he becomes inattentive, withdrawn, or frustrated.

Physical Development, Including Motor and Sensory Development

It is important for the teacher to be aware of the physical stages of development and how the child's physical growth affects the child's learning. In general, a child's physical abilities develop downward, from head to toe, and outward from the torso or central body mass to the extremities. In normal development, both gross motor (large body movements) and fine motor (small, precise body movements) develop together.

From an educational standpoint, children are generally assumed to have met the following gross motor milestones by the time they enter first grade:

- Locomotion such as hopping, running, skipping, jumping, and sliding

- Alternating or moving from one gross motor activity to another in a regular pattern

- Motor activities with an object or ball, such as kicking, throwing, or catching

- Motor activities involving simple tumbling exercises, such as somersaults

- Moving to a simple rhythm or beat

Fine motor skills considered necessary for success in first grade include such things as:

- Establishment of hand dominance

- "Pincer grasp" or using finger(s) and thumb to pinch something

- Some variation of the "tripod grasp" of a pencil or writing implement

- Ability to cut out large, irregular patterns in paper

- Ability to draw a reasonable representation of a circle, square, triangle, person (with legs, arms, face) and a house

- Ability to use both hands jointly for a task such as unscrewing a lid or putting two Lego blocks together

- Assembling large interlocking puzzle pieces

- Clothing skills such as buttoning , unbuttoning and tying shoelaces

In addition to motor disorders, individuals with physical disabilities may have multidisabling conditions such as concomitant hearing impairments, visual impairments, perceptual disorders, speech defects, behavior disorders, or mental handicaps, performance, and emotional responsiveness.

Cognitive Development

Children go through patterns of learning, beginning with preoperational thought processes, and then moving on to concrete operational thoughts. Eventually, they begin to acquire the mental ability to think about and solve problems in their heads because they can manipulate objects symbolically. Even when children reach a stage where they can use symbols such as words and numbers to represent objects and relations, they will persist in needing concrete reference points for some time. It is essential that children be encouraged to use and develop the thinking skills they possess in solving problems that interest them. The content of the curriculum must be relevant, engaging, and meaningful to the students.

Some common features indicating a progression from more simple to more complex cognitive development include the following:

Children (ages 6-12)

Children begin to develop the ability to think in concrete ways. Concrete operations are those performed in the presence of the object and events that are to be used. Examples include knowing how to combine (addition), separate (subtract or divide), order (alphabetize and sort/categorize), and transform objects and actions (change things such as 25 pennies to 1 quarter).

Adolescents (ages 12-18)

Adolescence marks the beginning of the development of more complex thinking skills, including abstract thinking, the ability to reason from known principles (form own new ideas or questions), the ability to consider many points of view according to varying criteria (compare or debate ideas or opinions), the ability to see things from different perspectives, and the ability to think about the process of thinking. The transition from concrete thinking to formal logical operations occurs over time. Each adolescent progresses at varying rates in developing his or her ability to think in more complex ways and develops his or her own view of the world. Some adolescents may be able to apply logical operations to schoolwork long before they are able to apply them to personal dilemmas. When emotional issues arise, they often interfere with an adolescent's ability to think in more complex ways. The ability to consider possibilities as well as facts may influence decision making in either positive or negative ways.

SKILL 1.2 **Theoretical approaches to student learning and motivation**

No two students are alike, so it follows that no students *learn* alike. To apply a one-dimensional instructional approach is to impose learning limits on students. A teacher must acknowledge the variety of learning styles and abilities among students, and apply multiple instructional methods to ensure that every child has appropriate opportunities to master the subject matter, demonstrate such mastery, and improve learning skills with each lesson.

Differentiated Instruction

In recent years, increasing emphasis has been put on incorporating at least some principles of differentiated instruction into classrooms with students of mixed ability. Tomlinson (2001) states that teachers must first determine where the students are with reference to an objective, *then* tailor specific lesson plans and learning activities to help each student learn as much as possible about that objective. The effective teacher seeks to connect all students to the subject matter through multiple techniques, with the goal that each student will relate to one or more techniques and excel in the learning process. This is particularly relevant to instruction of students with disabilities. Differentiated instruction encompasses modifying curriculum in several areas.

- Content: What is the teacher going to teach? Or, perhaps better put, what does the teacher want the students to learn? Differentiating content means that students have access to aspects of the content that pique their interest, with a complexity that provides an appropriate challenge to their intellectual development, but does not go beyond their frustration level.

- Process: The classroom management techniques through which instructional organization and delivery are maximized for the diverse student group. These techniques should include dynamic, flexible grouping activities, where instruction and learning occur as whole-class, teacher-led activities and in a variety of small group settings, such as teacher-guided small group, peer learning and teaching (while teacher observes and coaches), or independent centers or pairs.

- Product: The expectations and requirements placed on students to demonstrate their knowledge or understanding. The type of product expected from each student should reflect that student's own capabilities.

Promoting Motivation

Before instruction begins, meaningful and relevant activities should be chosen, and should be appropriately leveled in terms of difficulty. This is particularly effective for students with disabilities, who are more likely to act out when demands are beyond their ability to meet. Teacher behaviors that motivate students include:

- Maintain success expectations through teaching, goal setting, establishing connections between effort and outcome, and self-appraisal and reinforcement.

- Have a supply of intrinsic incentives such as rewards, appropriate competition between students, and the value of the academic activities.

- Focus on students' intrinsic motivation through adapting the tasks to students' interests, providing opportunities for active response, using a variety of tasks, providing rapid feedback, incorporating games into the lesson, and allowing students the opportunity to make choices, create, and interact with peers.

- For some students with disabilities, extrinsic rewards and token systems (prize charts, etc.) may be necessary. Often the student's IEP will specify use of such tools.

- Stimulate students' learning by modeling positive expectations and attributions. Project enthusiasm and personalize abstract concepts. Students will be better motivated if they know what they will be learning. The teacher should also model problem-solving and task-related thinking so students can see how the process is done.

For adolescents, motivation strategies are usually aimed at getting the student actively involved in the learning process. Since the adolescent has the opportunity to get involved in a wider range of activities outside the classroom (e.g., job, car, being with friends), stimulating motivation may be the focus even more than academics.

Motivation may be improved by allowing the student a degree of choice in what is being taught or how it will be taught. The teacher will, if possible, obtain a commitment either through a verbal or written contract between the student and the teacher. Adolescents also respond to regular feedback, especially when that feedback shows they are making progress.

SKILL 1.3 Basic characteristics and defining factors for each of the major disability categories

The previous classification system is useful when defining eligibility for special services and placement in special service programs. The following tables demonstrate traits and characteristics of "Specific Learning Disabilities" and "Diagnoses of Children with Special Needs." It is important for the teacher to understand the terminology of these disabilities when applied to his or her students.

SPECIFIC LEARNING DISABILITIES	
Central Auditory Processing Deficit (CAPD)	Students with CAPDs have normal hearing *physiologically*, but have deficits in the processing or auditory input. Such deficits impact both cognitive and linguistic functioning in both receptive and expressive modes. The symptoms sometimes are mistaken for ADHD because the child cannot adequately process instructions and information.
Communication Disorders	This group includes deficits in language processing, articulation, fluency, or voice.
Dyscalculia	Any serious disability in processing mathematical information, concepts, or calculations, particularly when there are not corresponding disabilities in other verbal skills.
Dysgraphia	A serious deficit in the ability to carry out the motor or cognitive functions necessary to write. This may be a motor problem and/or a cognitive inability to plan and generate sentences. It is usually neurologically based.

Continued on next page

Dyslexia	Although this term is not as widely used as it once was, it still refers to a reading disability that is based in problems learning to associate sounds and symbols (letters).
Nonverbal Learning Disabilities	These disabilities impact many areas of nonverbal problem solving. Although children with them can often "read" and memorize well, they have significant difficulty understanding what they read, as well as difficulty understanding nonverbal communication such as facial expressions and body language. As a result, both social competence and emotional well-being can be impacted. There may also be deficits in visual-spatial organization and motor control.
Pervasive Developmental Disorders Not Otherwise Specified (PDDNOS)	These disorders are very similar to autism and are sometimes referred to as "autism spectrum disorders." Though children with these disorders do not qualify as autistic, they have many of the same deficits in social and communication skills.

In addition to specific learning disabilities, special education teachers may often encounter the following diagnoses of children with special needs.

DIAGNOSES OF CHILDREN WITH SPECIAL NEEDS	
Attention Deficit Disorder (ADD) or Attention Deficit with Hyperactivity Disorder (ADHD)	Children with these disorders display serious inattention, distractibility, disorganization, and poor impulse control, often with constant movement or activity they cannot control. Typically, they do not show delayed cognition or mental retardation. These disorders can often accompany other medical or learning disorders, however, and further impact learning.
Asperger's Syndrome	Although the definition of this disorder is changing in some quarters, it usually refers to a type of autism involving most of the characteristics of autism, without cognitive delay or retardation. Children with this disorder have normal or above average cognitive abilities. It is often referred to as a "high functioning form of autism."
Cerebral Palsy	This is a neurological disorder that involves damage to the motor centers of the brain (during fetal development, or during or after birth) and results in tremors and muscle weakness or tension. Both gross and fine motor skills can be affected.
Developmental Disabilities	These disabilities result in significant delays in physical (e.g., Cerebral Palsy) or cognitive (mental retardation) abilities.
Tourette Syndrome	This is a seizure disorder (not epilepsy) that produces motor, vocal, and other tics (i.e., highly repetitive actions) over which the child has minimum control.

See Skill 5.1 for Federal Definitions.

SKILL 1.4 Impact of disabilities on individuals, families, and society across the life span

An exceptionality may have a positive, negative, or neutral effect throughout a child's life, depending on the characteristics of the exceptionality, available resources, and support system.

Early Childhood

Often the life of a child with an exceptionality will be different beginning at birth. The child may experience marked developmental delays in some areas and not in other areas. The child's exceptionality may have negative and positive effects on siblings. Some siblings may have feelings of embarrassment, resentfulness, or even guilt related to their sibling with a disability. Other siblings may gain insight, tolerance, and appreciation because of their experience with the sibling with the exceptionality.

The child with the exceptionality may require special diets, transportation, medical care, and other special services. These requirements may cause financial stress on the family.

School Age

Academic and social skills are crucial at this age. The goal during this age is to prepare the child to be an independent, productive citizen. A child with an exceptionality may or may not experience a difficult time interacting with others. If these skills are not taught, this deficiency may cause the child difficulty in developing relationships and future employment problems.

Having an exceptionality may or may not limit a child's academic ability. The goal of the educational system is to include students with exceptionalities in the general education curriculum as much as possible. The degree of inclusion in the curriculum is based on each student's ability.

In the teen years, when young people are beginning to express their individuality, the very appearance of walking into a special education classroom can bring feelings of inadequacy, as well as labeling by peers that the student is "special." Being considered normal is the desire of almost all individuals with disabilities, regardless of the age or disability. People with disabilities today, as many years ago, still measure their successes by how their achievements mask or hide their disabilities.

During this time in life, the student and other concerned individuals collaborate to decide on the child's future and how the student will transition into the next phase of life. Depending on the characteristics of the child's exceptionality, it may be decided that the student will attend technical school, attend post-secondary education, or begin working.

Adult

An adult with an exceptionality may or may not lead a life that is different from any other adult. The adult may go to work every day and come home to take care of all of his or her own needs. Another adult with an exceptionality may live with a caregiver. Adults with exceptionalities have various living options, ranging from residential homes to a very restricted environment, such as institutions.

Many outside agencies provide services for those adults who may need assistance.

Some adults may still lack social skills to maintain a healthy work environment; therefore, job coaches, mentors, or outside agencies are needed to provide additional assistance or needed work skills.

Adults who lack social skills may also have difficulty finding mates and may never have families, while others may find mates and raise families of their own with no outside assistance.

SKILL 1.5 **Impact of language, cultural, and gender differences on the identification process**

Students are more than the sum of the effects of their disabilities. Cultural, linguistic, and gender characteristics also help define the student, and these characteristics must be taken into account for instructional planning.

Just as cultures place varying values on education and the role of genders, different views may also be taken of individuals with disabilities, including appropriate education, career goals, and the individual's role in society. The special needs educator must first become familiar with the cultural representations of the students and the community in which he or she teaches. As the special needs educator demonstrates respect for each individual student's culture, he or she will build the rapport necessary to work with the student, family, and community to prepare the student for future productive work, independence, and possible post-secondary education or training (IDEA 2004).

The educational experience for most students is a complex experience with a diversity of interlocking meanings and inferences. If one aspect of the complexity is altered, it affects other aspects, which may have an impact on how a student or teacher views an instructional or learning experience. With the current demographic profile of today's school communities, the complexity of understanding, interpreting, and synthesizing nuances from the diversity of cultural lineages can provide many communication and learning impediments that could hamper the acquisition of learning, especially for students with exceptionalities.

Teachers must create **PERSONALIZED LEARNING COMMUNITIES** where every student is a valued member of and contributor to the classroom experiences. In classrooms where sociocultural attributes of the student population are incorporated into the fabric of the learning process, dynamic interrelationships are created that enhance the learning experience and the personalization of learning.

Similarly, inclusion of students with exceptionalities into the general education classroom can be beneficial for advanced academic achievement as well as sociocultural development, provided proper accommodations for their special needs are made. Researchers continue to show that personalized learning environments increase learning for students, decrease drop-out rates among marginalized students, and decrease unproductive student behavior that can result from constant cultural misunderstandings or miscues between students.

Learning environments that help children with and without disabilities understand that both learning abilities and styles differ, and that each child has a place in and something to contribute to the group can prevent misunderstandings and intolerance of students with special needs. Promoting diversity of learning and cultural competency in the classroom creates a world of multicultural opportunities and learning. When students are able to step outside their comfort zones and share the world of a homeless student or empathize with an English language learner (ELL) who has just immigrated to the United States, is learning English for the first time, and is still trying to keep up with the academic learning in an unfamiliar language, then students grow exponentially in social understanding and cultural connectedness.

Personalized learning communities provide supportive learning environments that address the academic and emotional needs of all students. As sociocultural knowledge is conveyed continuously in the interrelated experiences shared cooperatively and collaboratively in student groupings and individualized learning, the current and future benefits will continue to present the case and importance of understanding the whole child, inclusive of the social and cultural context.

> **PERSONALIZED LEARNING COMMUNITIES:** every student is a valued member of and contributor to the classroom experiences

> *When students with exceptionalities are provided with numerous academic and social opportunities to share cultural approaches to learning, everyone in the classroom benefits from bonding through shared experiences and an expanded viewpoint of a world experience that vastly differs from their own.*

Gender

More boys are identified as having emotional and behavioral problems, especially hyperactivity and attention deficit disorder, autism, childhood psychosis, and problems with poor control (aggression, socialized aggression). Girls, on the other hand, have more problems with overcontrol (withdrawal and phobias). Problems with mental retardation and language and learning disabilities are much more prevalent in boys than in girls.

Gender may also create sensitive issues, since some cultures and sub-cultural groups have very specific and distinct ideas about appropriate male and female roles in society. These ideas may impact what is considered an appropriate functional skill. Some cultural groups, for example, consider family food preparation and cooking to be appropriate skills for women, but not for men. Regardless of whether the teacher agrees with a view or not, it is the teacher's responsibility to take it into consideration when designing instruction. In all cases, the planned method of instruction, as well as any materials used, must be culturally sensitive, as well as practically effective.

SKILL 1.6 Co-occurring conditions

Children who have multiple disabilities are an extremely heterogeneous population. Their characteristics are determined by the type and severity of their combined disabilities; therefore, they differ in their sensory, motor, social, and cognitive abilities. Although any number of combinations of disabilities is possible, major dimensions typically include mental retardation, neurological impairments, emotional disturbance, or deafness and blindness. Those whose impairments combine to form multiple disabilities often exhibit characteristics on a severe level. Low self-esteem and poor social skills often characterize this population. Youngsters with severe disabilities may possess profound language or perceptual-cognitive deprivations. Moreover, they may have extremely fragile physiological conditions. "It is important to understand that (with) the problem of severe/profound disabilities…It is the extent of the disabilities that results in the child's classification, not the type of disabilities" (Blackhurst & Berdine, 1985, pp. 473–474).

Some characteristics students with severe or profound multidisabilities have are:

- Often not toilet trained

- Frequently nonambulatory

- Aggressiveness toward others without provocation and antisocial behavior

- Markedly withdrawn or unresponsive to others

- No attention to even the most pronounced social stimuli

- Self-mutilation (head banging, biting, and scratching or cutting of self)

- Rumination (self-induced vomiting, swallowing vomitus)

- Self-stimulation (rocking, hand-flapping)

- Intense temper tantrums of unknown origin

- Excessive, pointless imitation, or the total absence of the ability to imitate

- Inability to be controlled verbally

- Extremely brittle medical existence (life-threatening conditions such as congenital heart disease, respiratory difficulties, metabolic disorders, central nervous system disorders, and digestive malfunctions)

There are times when an exceptional student has a disability coupled with a behavioral issue. In order to tackle the issue of behavior problems, educators usually start with a Behavior Intervention Plan (BIP). One of the first steps to developing a BIP entails taking a detailed **FUNCTIONAL BEHAVIOR ASSESSMENT (FBA)** summary, which must define behaviors in observable and measurable terms along four variables: frequency, duration, intensity, and degree of severity.

FUNCTIONAL BEHAVIOR ASSESSMENT (FBA): defines behaviors in observable and measurable terms along four variables: frequency, duration, intensity, and degree of severity

The FBA must note the frequency of the behaviors that have been identified. Frequency consists of how often a behavior occurs in a specified time block (e.g. morning, afternoon, evening). The activity during which the behavior typically occurs is also recorded. For example, does it occur during lunch, transitions, group time, or another time period? The data should indicate the frequency of the individual behaviors and note when it is less frequent and when the behavior is most likely to occur.

The FBA can help identify the following:

- When the behavior was first observed and key events at that time

- Any signs or cues from the student that help predict that the behavior will occur

- What happens just before the behavior that may trigger the behavior

- Settings, situations, and other variables that influence the behavior

These observations should include the following:

- Specific days or time of day

- Specific settings such as school, home, class, hallway, or bus

- Particular subject areas such as math or P.E.

- Type or length of assignment

- The manner of presenting instruction, feedback, or corrections

- The particular person presenting the information

Another variable that must be addressed is the duration of the behaviors. This variable entails measuring how long the behavior takes place by timing the behavior from start to finish and writing it down.

A third variable that must be measured is the intensity of the behavior. The FBA must have a scale that assesses whether the behavior is of low, medium, or high intensity. If the student is having a tantrum, is there a scale to measure the intensity of the tantrum? For example, a highly intense tantrum might include hitting the teacher or classmates, while a less intense tantrum may include property damage.

A fourth variable that is measured when assessing behavior is the degree of severity. All behaviors can be put into different categories depending on their impact. More severe behavior problems would involve physical violence and destruction of property while less severe problems will involve screaming, yelling, and general disruption of class time.

The FBA may also include factors such as:

- When, where, and with whom the behavior is least likely to occur

- Specific skill deficits that interfere with the student's ability to behave as expected

- Whether the student is aware of expected behavior and understands the consequences of the behavior

- Whether the student has the skills necessary to behave as expected

- The apparent function of undesirable behavior (what the student gets, avoids, or escapes due to the behavior)

- Potential reinforcers for the student

SKILL 1.7 How family systems contribute to the development of individuals with disabilities

The special needs educator should be knowledgeable of family systems, as well as the impact of the systems on a family's response and contribution to the education of a child with special needs. The family systems theory, as outlined in the Bowen

For more on the
Bowen Center for the
Study of the Family,
see:

www.thebowencenter.org
/pages/ theory.html

Center for the Study of the Family, has been developed by Murray Bowen in recent decades. The Bowen Theory of Family Systems is outlined as follows:

- Triangles: Refer to the impact on existing relationships between two people in a family when a third individual joins the family. In the case of a child with a disability, it could refer to the impact of the child's needs and associated physical, emotional, and financial stress on the marriage of the parents.

- Differentiation of Self: Refers to the influence of family members to think alike and the individual's ability to think critically and independently while realizing the extent of his or her need for others.

- Nuclear Family Emotional System: Describes four basic relationship patterns that can develop or worsen because of tension. The patterns are marital conflict, dysfunction in one spouse, impairment of one or more children, and emotional distance.

- Family Projection Process: Refers to the parental projection of a perception (such as low self-esteem) or problem (learning disability) that results in the treatment of the child as such. With time, the projection may become a self-fulfilling prophecy.

  The projection process follows three steps:

  A. The parent focuses on a child out of fear that something is wrong with him or her

  B. The parent interprets the child's behavior as confirming the fear

  C. The parent treats the child as if something is really wrong

- Multigenerational Transmission Process: Refers to the impact of parenting and the resulting differentiation of self on future generations. In the case of the parents of a child with a disability, parents who have developed a stronger differentiation of self are more likely to acknowledge their child's disability (regardless of extended family perception of the social stigma it may bring) and to consider all options of treatment and educational programming for their child.

- Emotional Cutoff: Occurs when the individual distances him or herself from the family as an adult due to unresolved conflict. In the case of a child with a disability, a parent may distance him or herself from his or her own parents because of their ongoing opinion that the child with a severe disability should be institutionalized.

- Sibling Position: Is when birth order reflects tendencies of children in later interactions. Firstborn children tend to be leaders; younger siblings tend to be followers.

- **Societal Emotional Process:** Refers to the carryover of the above systems into all areas of personal interaction in the society (including the workplace and school).

The special needs educator should be aware of these systems as he or she interacts with families on a regular basis and communicates with them regarding IEP planning and considerations.

It is also important to remember, when interacting with families, culture and belief systems will have an impact on parental concerns and opinions about a child with a disability. For example, many mainstream American families would list future independence as a goal for a child with a disability. They hope that even a child with a severe disability will be able to live and work as independently as possible. However, from some cultural perspectives this goal would be unthinkable. It is the educator's responsibility to learn as much as possible about the family and the parental views on matters relevant to the child's education, and to listen carefully to the parents' views.

SKILL 1.8 Environmental and societal influences on student development and achievement

Though society has "progressed," and many things are more acceptable today than they were in years past, having a disability still carries a stigma. Historically, people with disabilities have been ostracized from their communities. Up until the 1970s, a large number of people with special needs were institutionalized at birth because their relatives either did not know what to do, they felt embarrassed to admit they had a child with a disability, or they gave in to the cultural peer pressure to put their "problem" away. Even today, one of the most detrimental attitudes about people with disabilities is that they are unable to contribute to society.

Nevertheless, the regular education classroom teacher now learns to accept and teach students with special needs. America's media today provide education and frequent exposure of people with special needs. Often, those with special needs who appear in media such as television and movies are generally those who rise above their "label" as disabled because of an extraordinary skill. Most people in the community are portrayed as accepting the "disabled" person only once that special skill is noted. Those who continue to express revulsion or prejudice toward the person with a disability often express remorse when the special skill is noted or if peer pressure becomes too intense. This portrayal often ignores those with learning and emotional disabilities who appear normal by appearance and who often feel and suffer from the prejudices.

DOMAIN II
PLANNING AND THE LEARNING ENVIRONMENT

PERSONALIZED STUDY PLAN

✗ **KNOWN MATERIAL/ SKIP IT**

PAGE	SKILL		KNOWN MATERIAL/ SKIP IT
27	2.1:	Characteristics of good lesson plans	☐
	2.2:	Basic elements of effective lesson plans	☐
	2.3:	Learning objectives that are measureable and appropriately challenging	☐
	2.4:	Means of providing access to the curriculum	☐
	2.5:	Organizing the learning environment	☐
	2.6:	Understanding how to manage student behavior	☐
	2.7:	Theory and practice of effective classroom management	☐
	2.8:	Design and maintenance of a safe and supportive classroom environment that promotes student achievement	☐

SKILL 2.1 Characteristics of good lesson plans

Well-formed lesson plans have measurable outcomes and definitive learning standards. Assessment information, once gathered, can be used to provide performance-based criteria and academic expectations for all students and to evaluate whether students have learned the expected skills and content of a subject area.

Instructional decisions and the lesson plan basis should include all aspects of the following:

- **Classroom Organization:** The teacher can vary grouping arrangements (e.g., large group, small group, peer tutoring, or learning centers) and methods of instruction (teacher-directed, student-directed) to enhance his or her lesson plan.

- **Classroom Management:** The teacher can vary grading systems, vary reinforcement systems, and vary the rules (differentiated for some students) accordingly when surveying the group of students he or she will be planning for.

- **Methods of Presentation/Variation of Methods Utilized:**

  1. Content—amount to be learned, time to learn, and concept level

  2. General Structure—advance organizers, immediate feedback, memory devices, and active involvement of students

  3. Type of Presentation—verbal or written, transparencies, audiovisual

- **Methods of Practice:**

  1. General Structure—amount to be practiced, time to finish, group, individual or teacher-directed, and varied level of difficulty

  2. Level of Response—copying, recognition, or recall with and without cues

  3. Types of Materials—worksheets, audiovisual, texts

- **Methods of Testing/Measureable Lesson Plan Outcomes:**

  1. Type—verbal, written, or demonstration

  2. General Structure—time to complete, amount to complete, group or individual testing

  3. Level of response—multiple choice, essay, recall of facts

In their book on research-based teaching strategies, Saphier, et al. (2008) describe research showing that the amount of time actually spent on "instruction is directly tied to classroom organization and management skills" (p. 52). If the teacher must delay or interrupt instruction to locate materials, boot up an assistive technology device, copy an extra worksheet, etc., then it is the *teacher*, not the student, who is "off-task."

This goes beyond simply having commonly used supplies (e.g., pencils, paper, and textbooks) available to students in accessible locations. It is essential that the teacher actually *plan* for the setup and organization of materials and that this organization reflects the nature of the lesson and the specific needs of students with disabilities. The teacher might, for example, have a table with each lesson's supplies set up in a specific spot. The arrangement will differ depending upon the type of lesson. A reading discussion might require a small group seated at a horse-shoe table near a table holding a variety of phonics materials, while an interactive science lesson might need experimental materials, recording sheets, and so forth, set up near a sink.

For students with disabilities, it may help to have visual pictures of the materials they are to bring or set up for each lesson (e.g., a picture of pencil, phonics folder, dry erase marker and board under the heading: "Phonics Practice" or math book, pencil, paper, and manipulatives under the "Math" heading). Any additional accommodations prescribed by individual students' IEPs should also be at hand (e.g., if Bobby needs a fiddle object or Pat needs a magnifying glass or window card for tracking, these should be *right there* when class begins).

SKILL 2.2 Basic elements of effective lesson plans

Teaching was once seen as developing lesson plans, teaching, going home early, and taking the summer off. However, the demands of a classroom involve much more than grading papers. National and state learning standards must be taken into account because not only will the teacher and students be measured by the students' scores at the end of the year, the school will also be graded. Teachers must be knowledgeable about state and local standards and skilled at structuring their own classes in ways that will meet those frameworks.

On the large scale, the teacher must think about the scope of his or her plans for the day, the week, the unit, the semester, and the year. The teacher must decide on the subject matter for the unit, semester, and year, making certain that it is appropriate to the age of the students, relevant to their real lives, and in their realm of anticipated interest. Should the teacher introduce politically controversial issues or avoid them? He or she must make these decisions deliberatively on the basis of feedback from students and, at the same time, keep sight of his or her objectives.

The chosen curriculum should introduce information in a cumulative sequence and not introduce too much new information at a time. Review difficult material and practice to aid retention. New vocabulary and symbols should be introduced one at a time, and the relationships of components to the whole should be stressed. Students' background information should be recalled to connect new information to the old. Finally, teach strategies or algorithms first and then move on to tasks that are more difficult.

Emergent Curriculum

EMERGENT CURRICULUM describes the projects and themes that classrooms embark on that have been inspired by the children's interests. This approach can be useful in overall curriculum design. Teachers use all the tools of assessment available to discover as much as they can about their students, and then continually assess the students throughout the unit or semester. As the teachers get to know the students, they listen to what their interests are and create a curriculum in response to what they learn from observations of their own students.

Webbing is a recent concept related to the idea of emergent curriculum. The two main uses are planning and recording curriculum. PLANNING WEBS are used to generate ideas for activities and projects for the children from an observed interest such as rocks. Teachers can work together to come up with ideas and activities for the children and to record them in a web format. Activities can be grouped by different areas of the room or by developmental domains. For example, clusters fall either under areas such as dramatic play or science areas or around domains such as language, cognitive, and physical development. Either configuration works; being consistent in each web is important. This format will work as a unit, weekly, or monthly program plan. Any new activities that emerge throughout the unit can also be added to the web. The record will serve in the future to plan activities that emerge from the children's play and ideas.

Lesson Plan Development

Lesson plans are important in guiding instruction in the classroom. Incorporating the nuts and bolts of a teaching unit, the LESSON PLAN outlines the steps of teacher implementation and assessment of the teacher's instructional effectiveness and student learning success. Teachers are able to objectify and quantify learning goals and targets in terms of incorporating effective performance-based assessments and projected criteria for identifying when a student has learned the

EMERGENT CURRICU-LUM: projects and themes that classrooms embark on that have been inspired by the children's interests

PLANNING WEBS: used to generate ideas for activities and projects for the children from an observed interest such as rocks

LESSON PLAN: outlines the steps of teacher implementation and assessment of the teacher's instructional effectiveness and student learning success

material presented. All components of a lesson plan—including the unit description, learning targets, learning experiences, explanation of learning rationale, and assessments—must be present to provide both quantifiable and qualitative data to ascertain whether student learning has taken place and whether effective teaching has occurred for the students.

Effective lesson plans will generally include the following in some form:

- Quizzes or reviews of the previous lesson

- Step-by-step presentations with multiple examples

- Guided practice and feedback

- Independent practice that requires the student to produce faster, increasingly independent (reduced scaffolding) responses

A typical format for a written lesson plan describing what is being taught and how the students will be able to access the information would include the following items:

1. **Unit description:** Describes the learning and classroom environment.

   A. **Classroom characteristics:** Describe the physical arrangements of the classroom and the student grouping patterns for the lesson being taught. Classroom rules and consequences should be clearly posted and visible.

   B. **Student characteristics:** Demographics of the classroom that include student number, gender, and cultural and ethnic backgrounds and students with IEPs.

2. **Learning goals, targets, and objectives:** What are the expectations of the lessons? Are the learning goals appropriate to the state learning standards and district academic goals? Are the targets appropriate for the grade level and subject content area and inclusive of a multicultural perspective and global viewpoint?

3. **Learning experiences for student:** How will student learning be supported using the learning goals?

   A. What prior knowledge or experiences will the students bring to the lesson? How will you check and verify that student knowledge?

   B. How will you engage all students in the classroom? How will students who have been identified as marginalized in the classroom be engaged in the lesson unit?

   C. How will the lesson plan be modified for students with IEPs, and how will independent education students be evaluated for learning and processing the modified lesson targets?

D. How will the multicultural aspect be incorporated into the lesson plan?

E. What interdisciplinary connections will be used to incorporate other subject areas?

F. What types of assessments and evaluations will be used to test student understanding and processing of the lesson plan?

G. How will students be cooperatively grouped to engage in the lesson?

4. Rationales for learning experiences: Provide data on how the lesson plan addresses student learning goals and objectives. Address whether the lesson provides accommodations for students with IEPs and provides support for marginalized students in the classroom.

5. Assessments: Construct pre- and post-assessments that evaluate student learning as it correlates to the learning goals and objectives. Do the assessments include a cultural integration that addresses the cultural needs and inclusion of students? Do assessments incorporate accommodations needed by students with special needs?

In designing lesson plans teachers should keep the following principles in mind:

Vary assignments
A variety of assignments on the same content allows students to match learning styles and preferences with the assignment. If all assignments are writing assignments, for example, students who are hands-on or visual learners are at a disadvantage unrelated to the content base itself.

Cooperative learning
COOPERATIVE LEARNING activities allow students to share ideas, expertise, and insight in a non-threatening setting. The focus tends to remain on positive learning rather than on competition.

Structured environment
Some students need and benefit from clear structure that defines the expectations and goals of the teacher. The student knows what is expected and when and can work and plan accordingly.

Clearly stated assignments
Assignments should be clearly stated along with the expectation and criteria for completion. Reinforcement and practice activities should not be a guessing game for the students. Many students with special needs benefit from written, step-by-step instructions and printed rubrics they can use to check off their tasks as they

COOPERATIVE LEARNING: activities that allow students to share ideas, expertise, and insight in a non-threatening setting; the focus tends to remain on positive learning rather than on competition

STRUCTURED ENVIRONMENT: an environment in which the expectations and goals of the teacher are clearly defined; the student knows what is expected and when and can work and plan accordingly

proceed. The exception is, of course, those situations in which a discovery method is used.

Independent practice

INDEPENDENT PRACTICE: allowing a student to work independently so that the teacher can assess his or her performance

INDEPENDENT PRACTICE involving application and repetition is necessary for thorough learning. These activities should always be within the student's abilities to perform successfully without assistance. Students with special needs often benefit from **STAGED INDEPENDENT PRACTICE**, where the teacher provides scaffolding to start, then gradually fades out the support until the student is working as independently as possible.

Repetition

STAGED INDEPENDENT PRACTICE: an approach to student activities in which the teacher provides scaffolding to start, then gradually fades out the support until the student is working as independently as possible

Very little learning is successful with a single exposure. Learners generally require multiple exposures to the same information for learning to take place. However, this repetition does not have to be dull and monotonous. Varied assignments can provide repetition of content or skill practiced without repetition of specific activities. This method helps keep learning fresh and exciting for the student.

Overlearning

OVERLEARNING: a principle of effective learning that recommends students continue to study and review after they have achieved initial mastery

As a principle of effective learning, **OVERLEARNING** recommends that students continue to study and review after they have achieved initial mastery. The use of repetition in the context of varied assignments offers the means to help students pursue and achieve overlearning. Many students with learning and memory disabilities will have some form of overlearning prescribed in their IEPs.

Methods of presentation of subject matter

The teacher can vary the method of presentation of new material in many ways depending upon the specific needs of the students. In general, subject matter should be presented in a fashion that helps students organize, understand, and remember important information. Students with learning disabilities will often benefit from hands-on, multimodal presentation and interaction with new concepts and materials. It is helpful if the goal of the lesson and the most important points are clearly stated at the start. Students with learning disabilities also benefit from material that is presented one concept at a time (this reduces cognitive demand). Advance organizers and other instructional devices can

- Connect information to what is already known (increases context)

- Make abstract ideas more concrete (reduces cognitive demand)

- Capture students' interest in the material

- Help students organize the information and visualize the relationships (increases context and reduces demand)

Organizers can be visual aids—such as diagrams, tables, charts, and guides—or verbal cues that alert students to the nature and content of the lesson. Organizers may be used:

- **Before the lesson** to alert the student to the main point of the lesson, establish a rationale for learning, and activate background information

- **During the lesson** to help students organize information, keep focused on important points, and aid comprehension

- **At the close of the lesson** to summarize and remember important points

Examples of organizers include the following:

- Question and graphic-oriented study guide

- Concept diagramming: Students brainstorm a concept and organize information into three lists (always present, sometimes present, and never present).

- Semantic feature analysis: Students construct a table with examples of the concept in one column and important features or characteristics in the opposite column. This table can involve words, pictures, or even concrete objects as necessary to meet the individual student's needs.

- Semantic webbing: The concept (in word, picture, or object) is placed in the middle of the chart or chalkboard and relevant information is placed around it. Lines show the relationships. Color coding and letting students physically attach string or pipe cleaners to make the web can increase context and make the conceptual relationships more concrete.

- Memory (mnemonic) devices

- Diagrams, charts, and tables

Instructional materials

In many school systems the textbooks and primary instructional materials have been chosen by the school, though the teacher may also be able to select additional materials. Although specialized materials for certain special needs (e.g., large print or CDs for students with visual disabilities or dyslexia) may be available, it is usually necessary for the teachers to modify instructional materials and texts for their students with special needs. It may be necessary to enlarge the print on a worksheet or text not available in large print, or to provide additional diagrams or rearrange text on the page for students with organizational difficulties. Students with certain visual or writing difficulties may not be able to copy math problems from a book, or may need larger numbers or space for their work.

Though the specific modifications will depend upon individual student needs, one of the most common requirements will be finding or revising text for learners who cannot read at grade level or who have difficulty comprehending what they read in content areas such as science and social studies. The most common specific learning disabilities involve reading difficulties. In order for such students to have equal access to the grade level curriculum in content areas, it is often necessary to revise printed material so students can access it at their reading comprehension level. Whether selecting published materials or revising them for the students, these guidelines should be followed in order to increase context, reduce cognitive demand, and provide content material that students with learning disabilities can access.

- Avoid complex sentences with many relative clauses

- Avoid the passive tense

- Try to make the topic sentence the first sentence in a paragraph

- Make sure paragraphs have a concluding sentence that restates the topic sentence in another way

- Use simple, declarative sentences that have only one main idea or concept at a time

- Use simple, single syllable, concrete words rather than more complex words (e.g., "an arduous journey" should be "a hard trip")

- Eliminate nonessential information in favor of the main concepts necessary to teach

- Try to use only one tense in all the sentences

- Add diagrams and illustrations whenever possible and deliver information through labels rather than complete sentences

- Whenever possible, include multisensory elements and multimodalities in the presentation

- Avoid unfamiliar names and terms that will "tie up" the students' cognitive efforts (e.g., while the student is trying to figure out how to read the name "Aloicious" he or she will miss the point of the sentence; change the name to "Al")

Methods of practice and retention

Many of the common review and practice methods used in general education classrooms are suitable for students with special needs. Others will need modification. Each daily lesson should begin with a review of the important facts, rules, and concepts of the previous lesson. The review may incorporate questions from the teacher, a brief quiz, checking homework, and feedback on homework. On the basis of the students' responses to the questions, the teacher can adjust the instruction of the lesson to go over areas that were not mastered or retained.

Reviews of the lesson can also be in the in the form of a synopsis and teacher questioning at the end of the lesson to see whether the students have learned the material. At the beginning of the next day, if the teacher sees that the students responded correctly at the end of the previous lesson, but not in the day-after review, they may need to work on retention strategies. Students with certain learning disabilities may need to "overlearn" new material—that is, additional practice and review may be necessary for them. The teacher may need to alter the amount or content of material to be practiced (limit it to the most essential concepts or skills, for example), the time allowed for practice, or the methods used. Some students may have disabilities that impact their ability to recall information, for example, and their practice may need to involve recognition rather than recall. Many students with learning disabilities need heavy teacher scaffolding support when a skill or concept is first introduced. They may also need a more gradual reduction of scaffolding than their peers without disabilities in order to retain the information.

Homework provides review opportunities for independent practice. Review should be done on a daily basis, with weekly and monthly cumulative reviews to provide information on retention of knowledge and opportunities to "overlearn" the materials. It may be necessary to modify the homework assigned to students with learning disabilities. In many cases students with certain learning or emotional disabilities cannot handle the same level of homework as students without disabilities. In addition, parents may or may not have the skills necessary to help practice the highly specialized lessons some children with learning disabilities need (e.g., specialized phoneme awareness practice).

Students can also review and practice skills in peer tutoring, cooperative learning arrangements, and individual student seatwork. When errors are observed, teachers should find opportunities to teach the materials again. By immediately correcting the errors, the student is not inadvertently reinforced for the wrong process. Opportunities to reteach can also appear in student questions about present material that refer back to previous material.

Lesson Plan Collaboration

According to Walther-Thomas et al. (2000), ongoing professional development that provides teachers with opportunities to create effective instructional practice is vital and necessary. "A comprehensive approach to professional development is perhaps the most critical dimension of sustained support for successful program implementation." The inclusive approach incorporates learning programs that include all stakeholders in defining and developing high quality programs for students. The figure below shows how an integrated approach of stakeholders can provide the optimal learning opportunity for all students.

Integrated Approach to Learning

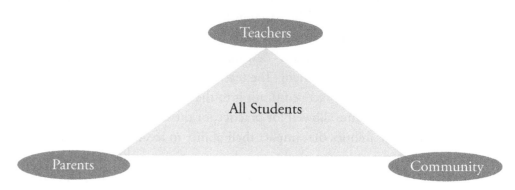

In this integrated approach to learning, teachers, parents, and community support become joint contributors to student learning. The focus and central core of the school community is triangular as a representation of how effective collaboration can work in creating success for student learners. The goal of student learning and achievement now becomes the heart of the school community.

For teachers, having a collaborative approach to instruction fosters for students a deeper appreciation of learning, subject matter, and knowledge acquisition. Implementing a consistent approach to learning from all stakeholders helps create equitable educational opportunities for all learners.

Research has shown that educators who collaborate become more diversified and effective in implementing curriculum and assessing effective instructional practices. Gaining additional insight into how students learn and modalities of differing learning styles can increase a teacher's capacity to develop effective instruction methods. Teachers who team teach or have daily networking opportunities can create a portfolio of curriculum articulation and inclusion for students.

People in business are always encouraged to network in order to further their careers. The same can be said for teaching. If English teachers get together and discuss what is going on in their classrooms, those discussions make the whole much stronger than the parts. Even if no formal opportunities for such networking exist, schools or even individual teachers should develop them and seek them out.

Learning objectives that are measureable and appropriately challenging

Creating Goals and Objectives

The teacher must be very skilled at writing academic objectives that fall within the guidelines of the state and local expectations. In addition, these objectives must be measurable so that, when the unit or semester is complete, he or she can know for sure whether or not goals have been met. Once long-range goals have been identified and established, the teacher must ensure that all goals and objectives are in conjunction with student ability and needs. Some objectives may be too basic for a higher level student, while others cannot be met with a student's current level of knowledge. There are many forms of evaluating student needs to ensure that all goals set are challenging, yet achievable.

The choice of instructional strategy depends primarily on the needs of the students. Teachers should check student cumulative files for reading level and prior subject area achievement. This analysis provides a basis for goal-setting but shouldn't be the only method used. Depending on the subject area, a basic skills test, reading level evaluations, writing samples, and interest surveys can all be useful in determining if all goals are appropriate. Informal observation throughout the year should be used to verify these more quantitative analyses. Finally, the teacher must take into consideration the student's level of motivation.

When students with disabilities are involved, information from their individualized education program or individualized family service plans can give the teacher guidelines on what type of instructional modifications are recommended for a particular child. Interviews with the student, when possible, and the student's family, as well as interest inventories can help the teacher select instructional strategies that students identify as helping them learn best. Interest inventories can be teacher-made, commercially prepared, or on computer programs. The teacher can construct a class profile from these inventories.

From the profiles, the teacher should be able to determine learning styles—whether the student is a visual, an auditory, or a kinesthetic learner. With a group of primarily visual learners, for example, a lecture would probably not be very effective unless it were accompanied by visual aids. Students also have preferences for certain types of materials over others, such as manipulative materials over worksheets. The cognitive level of the students will also affect the type of strategy employed.

Students who have difficulty with abstract concepts will need hands-on, concrete instruction strategies to help them make the transition from concrete to semi-concrete to abstract concepts. Using Cuisenaire rods to develop knowledge of fractions is an example of this method. In many classrooms, student abilities will vary and a differentiated form of instruction will be helpful.

A teacher may adapt an objective provided by the state or district in order to meet the needs of their student population. For example, a teacher might adapt the objective *"State five causes of World War II"* to require a higher level of cognitive demand or abstract thought by saying, *"State five causes of World War II and explain how they contributed to the start of the war."* The objective could be modified for a lower level of cognitive demand by saying, *"From a list of causes, pick three that specifically caused World War II."*

The type of task also influences choice of instructional strategy. Teaching a mnemonic device is effective in helping students remember the names of the planets in order, whereas an outline is more useful for reviewing a history chapter. Other factors influencing choice of strategy involve students' frustration level, motivation, and attitude towards the task. The need for supervision and assistance, the ability to work independently or in groups, and variations in time needed to complete the task also affect choice of strategy.

> *When organizing and sequencing objectives, remember that skills are building blocks. A taxonomy of educational objectives, such as that provided by Bloom, can be helpful in constructing and organizing objectives.*

When organizing and sequencing objectives, remember that skills are building blocks. A taxonomy of educational objectives, such as that provided by Bloom (1956), can be helpful in constructing and organizing objectives. Simple, factual knowledge of material is low on this cognitive taxonomy and should be worked with early in the sequence (for example, memorizing definitions or famous quotes). Eventually, objectives should be developed to include higher-level thinking such as comprehension (i.e., being able to use a definition); application (i.e., being able to apply the definition to other situations); synthesis (i.e., being able to add other information); and evaluation (i.e., being able to judge the value of something).

SKILL 2.4 Means of providing access to the curriculum

Accessing the curriculum requires special education teachers and related professionals to assess student needs. Each student is an individual and has a specific learning style. Individualized instruction and assessment reveals that each student obtains knowledge and learns content from the curriculum in various ways.

Multiple Intelligences

Some of the most prominent learning theories in education today have been influenced by brain-based learning research and the emergence of Multiple Intelligence Testing. Supported by recent brain research, these approaches suggest that knowledge about the way the brain retains information enables educators to design the most effective learning environments and to maximize curriculum access. Caine, et al. (2005) cite twelve principles that relate knowledge about the brain to teaching practices. These twelve principles are:

- The brain is a complex adaptive system
- The brain is social
- The search for meaning is innate
- We use patterns to learn more effectively
- Emotions are crucial to developing patterns
- Each brain perceives and creates parts and whole simultaneously
- Learning involves focused and peripheral attention
- Learning involves conscious and unconscious processes
- We have at least two ways of organizing memory
- Learning is developmental
- Complex learning is enhanced by challenge (and inhibited by threat)
- Every brain is unique (particularly relevant to teachers of students with special needs)

The **MULTIPLE INTELLIGENCES THEORY**, developed by Howard Gardner (1999), suggests that students learn in (at least) seven different ways. These include:

- Visually/spatially
- Musically
- Verbally
- Logically/mathematically
- Interpersonally
- Intrapersonally
- Bodily/kinesthetically

> **MULTIPLE INTELLIGENCES THEORY:**
> Howard Gardner's theory that students learn in at least seven different ways

Many students with disabilities find it particularly difficult to learn in a nonpreferred style, so identifying the preferred style can be crucial to the accommodations needed for a student with disabilities.

The Inclusion Movement

The **INCLUSION MOVEMENT** has had enormous impact on special education. In its purest form, this movement is based on the philosophy that all children with disabilities belong in a general education class, and that all must be accommodated and taught in that setting. This movement attracted many supporters who are both vocal and insistent about their beliefs. In many cases, the need for social integration of students with and without disabilities is at the heart of their concerns. Kirk, et al. (2003) list six beliefs central to this movement:

- ALL students belong in general education class—NO exceptions whatsoever

- General education teachers can and should teach all students including those with disabilities

- General education teachers will have all necessary supports to do this

- Quality education is a right, not a privilege

- Success, literacy, and graduation are a must for all students

- Alternative channels will be created for students who cannot otherwise succeed

> **INCLUSION MOVEMENT:** the philosophy that all children with disabilities belong in a general education class, and that all must be accommodated and taught in that setting

---

SKILL 2.5 Organizing the learning environment

In the education field, best practice is a term usually associated with work that is serious, thoughtful, and informed by current research in teaching and learning. Based on multidisciplinary research, some of the best practices that can be used in the educational setting include problem and project based learning; higher-order thinking; active, student-centered learning; collaboration; application of skill and knowledge; and student engagement. In special education, best practices also include a variety of additional tasks, such as aligning instruction with the IEP or 504 Plan and modifying various aspects of the educational environment and/or instruction to meet the special needs of the student.

The current educational reform efforts suggest that many teaching methods based on constructivist principles advance learning in students with special needs more effectively than teaching-by-telling. The social aspect of learning by collaboration and an individual's need to explore and experiment are best directed through instruction based on constructivist theory.

> *In special education, best practices include a variety of tasks, such as aligning instruction with the IEP or 504 Plan and modifying various aspects of the educational environment and/or instruction to meet the special needs of the student.*

Some of the constructivist-based strategies recognized as best practice include student-centered instruction, experiential and holistic learning, authentic experiences, reflective exercises, social interactions that scaffold learning, collaborative grouping, problem-oriented activities, integrated thematic units, and hands-on learning activities.

Using a mixture of these methods throughout the school year creates a balance of activities for students. These methods also help create a supportive classroom environment. In such an environment, students make choices, take risks comfortably, hold themselves accountable, express themselves in a number of ways, and establish a community of learners.

The most effective teaching environments are student-centered classrooms with an abundance of project-based activities and opportunities for collaboration and scaffolding support for learning strategies and skills. In order to promote problem solving and close the gap between inert knowledge and knowledge application, teachers must anchor instruction within an authentic context that will mirror real-life problems.

Another best practice occurs when teachers build a community of learners. Communities take part in activities together with a shared understanding about what they are doing and what it means to them. Members of the community have a chance to expand both the individual's and the group's knowledge, participate in decision making, take risks without fear of failure, develop expertise, experience a variety of activities, and work on tasks with others.

It is in the teacher's best interest to promote community-based learning in a structured, scheduled manner. Planning to structure the classroom experiences in advance is best, since aversive situations will be avoided. Thus, settings that stimulate the aggressive child to act out can be redesigned, and situations that stimulate group participation can be set up in advance for the child who acts in a withdrawn manner. Promoting a positive environment is critical.

One of the best practices used by technology-integrating teachers is focusing on the curriculum objectives and student disabilities or needs first and then deciding when and if to use technology to help students meet these objectives.

Scheduling the Day

Schedule development depends upon the type of class (elementary or secondary) and the setting (regular classroom or resource room). However, general rules of thumb apply to both types and settings.

1. Allow time for transitions, planning, and setups.

2. Aim for maximum instructional time by pacing the instruction quickly and allotting time for practice of the new skills.

3. Proceed from short assignments to long ones, breaking up long lessons or complex tasks into short sessions or step-by-step instruction.

4. Follow a less preferred academic or activity with a highly preferred academic or activity.

5. In settings where students are working on individualized plans, do not schedule all the students at once in activities that require a great deal of teacher assistance. For example, have some students work on math or spelling while the teacher works with the students in reading, which usually requires more teacher involvement.

6. Break up a longer segment into several smaller segments with a variety of activities.

7. When working with students with disabilities, it may be necessary to adjust the schedule to fit their best working times; some students take medicine that affects their ability to work, and the schedule must take this into account.

Special Considerations for Elementary Classrooms

1. Determine the amount of time that is needed for activities such as P.E., lunch, or recess.

2. Allow about fifteen to twenty minutes each for opening and closing exercises. Spend this time for such housekeeping activities as collecting lunch money, going over the schedule, cleaning up, reviewing the day's activities, and getting ready to go home.

3. Schedule concentrated academics for periods when the students are more alert and motivated (remember to pay attention to any medication schedules relevant to students with disabilities).

4. Build in time for slower students to finish their work; others may work at learning centers or other enrichment activities of interest. Allowing extra time gives the teacher time to give more attention where it is needed, conduct assessments, or for students to complete or correct work.

Special Considerations for Secondary Classes

Secondary school-days are usually divided into five, six, or seven periods of about fifty minutes, with time for homeroom and lunch. Students cannot stay behind and finish their work, since they have to leave for a different room. Resource room time should be scheduled so that the student does not miss academic instruction in his or her classroom or miss desirable nonacademic activities. In schools where special education teachers also co-teach or work with students in the regular classroom, the regular teacher will have to coordinate lesson plans with those of the special education teacher. Consultation time will also have to be budgeted into the schedule.

Organization and Distribution of Materials

Instructional momentum requires an organized system for material placement and distribution. Inability to find an overhead transparency, a necessary chart page, or the handout worksheet for the day not only stops the momentum, but is very irritating to students. Disorganization of materials frustrates both teacher and students. Effective teachers deal with daily classroom procedures efficiently and quickly so students spend the majority of class time engaged in academic tasks.

> Instructional momentum requires an organized system for material placement and distribution.

In the lower grades, an organized system often includes a "classroom helper" for effective distribution and collection of books, equipment, supplies, etc. Care must be taken when using such a system with students with some disabilities, however. Sometimes students can be so distracted by the demands of distributing or organizing materials that learning time is seriously reduced. The teacher must take individual student needs into account.

At higher grade levels, the teacher is concerned with materials such as textbooks, written instructional aids, worksheets, computer programs, etc., which must be produced, maintained, distributed, and collected for future use. One important consideration is the production of sufficient copies of duplicated materials to satisfy classroom needs. Another is the efficient distribution of worksheets and other materials. The teacher may decide to hand out materials as students are in their learning sites (desks, etc.) or to have distribution materials at a clearly specified place (or small number of places) in the classroom. In any case, teachers should have firmly established procedures, completely understood by students, for receiving classroom materials.

An effective teacher will also consider the needs and abilities of his or her students when developing routines or a daily schedule. For routines, a teacher might motivate a low-achieving student with a coveted task (such as taking down the attendance sheet or a recommendation for safety patrol) in order to increase confidence in that child. This increased confidence could lead to an increased interest in school and improved learning. Likewise, a teacher should also consider the needs of his or her students when developing the aspects of the daily schedule. For instance, if faced with a "hard to calm down" group, a teacher might schedule quiet reading time after recess. Being aware of their students' trends and characteristics in developing a classroom routine can significantly impact student learning.

Safety Provisions

Emergency response routines can present significant challenges to students with disabilities. Traditionally, the major emergency responses include two categories for student movement: tornado warning response and building evacuation (fire, bomb threat, etc.). More recently, many schools practice emergency procedures for building invasion, as well. For tornadoes, the prescribed response is to evacuate all students and personnel to the first floor of multi-story buildings and to place students along walls away from windows. All persons, including the teacher, should then crouch on the floor and cover their heads with their hands. These are standard procedures for severe weather, particularly tornadoes.

Most other emergency situations require evacuation of the school building. Teachers should be thoroughly familiar with evacuation routes established for each classroom in which they teach. Teachers should accompany and supervise students throughout the evacuation procedure and account for all students under their supervision. Teachers should then continue to supervise students until the building may be reoccupied (upon proper school or community authority) or until other procedures are followed for students to officially leave the school area and cease to be the supervisory responsibility of the school.

All these scenarios require extra care when working with students with disabilities. Some students have physical disabilities that must be taken into account in such emergencies. Others, such as autistic students, may react strongly to the sounds, sights, and routine disruption of even drills for such emergencies. Extra practice with students with special needs and a clear plan involving additional adult assistance must be in place. For example, the class might have an "emergency response team" that automatically comes to the room when such events—or drills for them—occur.

Homework

Mercer and Mercer recommend that homework be planned at the instructional level of the student and incorporated into the learning process of regular class work. The amount of work and length of time needed will vary according to age and grade level. The following are recommended times for students in regular education classes:

Primary Grades	Three 15-minute assignments per week
Grades 4 to 6	Two to four 15- to 45-minute assignments per week

Continued on next page

Grades 7 to 9	As many as five 45- to 75-minute assignments per week
Grades 10 to 12	As many as five 75- to 120-minute assignments per week

Homework assignments may need to be modified for some students with disabilities. Some students with disabilities may be unable to handle the usual amount of homework. Care should be taken to ensure that the homework practice is practice, not new learning. Like many aspects of instruction, homework should be differentiated.

Classroom Transition

TRANSITION refers to changes in class activities that involve movement. Examples are:

- Breaking up from large group instruction into small groups for learning centers and small group instructions

- Moving from the classroom to lunch, to the playground, or to elective classes

- Finishing reading at the end of one period and getting ready for math the next period

- Emergency situations such as fire drills

Effective teachers use class time efficiently. This efficiency results in higher student–subject engagement and will likely result in more subject matter retention. One way teachers use class time efficiently is through a smooth transition from one activity to another; this activity is also known as management transition. MANAGEMENT TRANSITION is when the teacher shifts from one activity to another in a systematic, academically oriented way. One factor that contributes to efficient management transition is the teacher's management of instructional material. Effective teachers gather their materials during the planning stage of instruction. Doing this, a teacher avoids flipping through items looking for the items necessary for the current lesson. Momentum is lost and student concentration is broken when this occurs.

In addition, teachers who keep students informed of the sequencing of instructional activities maintain systematic transitions because the students are prepared to move on to the next activity. For example, the teacher says, "When we finish with this guided practice together, we will turn to page twenty-three and each student will do the exercises. I will then circulate throughout the classroom helping on an individual basis. Okay, let's begin." Following an example such as this will lead to systematic smooth transitions between activities because the students will be turning to page twenty-three when the class finishes the practice

TRANSITION: changes in class activities that involve movement

MANAGEMENT TRANSITION: when the teacher shifts from one activity to another in a systematic, academically oriented way

Teachers who keep students informed of the sequencing of instructional activities maintain systematic transitions because the students are prepared to move on to the next activity.

without a break in concentration. These practices are particularly important for students with some disabilities. They may need extra time for transitions, or more advanced warning, or even a physical signal such as a bell or light, to help them manage the change.

Another method that leads to smooth transitions is to move students in groups and clusters rather than one by one. This is called group fragmentation. For example, if some students do seat work while other students gather for a reading group, the teacher moves the students in predetermined groups. Instead of calling the individual names of the reading group, which would be time-consuming and laborious, the teacher simply says, "Will the blue reading group please assemble at the reading station. The red and yellow groups will quietly do the vocabulary assignment I am now passing out." As a result of this activity, the classroom is ready to move on in a matter of seconds rather than minutes. Again, this can be particularly helpful for students with some disabilities, as they have the added context of their group's movement to help them figure out what to do next.

ACADEMIC TRANSITION SIGNALS: teacher utterance[s] that indicate movement of the lesson from one topic or activity to another by indicating where the lesson is and where it is going

The teacher may also employ **ACADEMIC TRANSITION SIGNALS**, which are teacher utterance[s] that indicate movement of the lesson from one topic or activity to another by indicating where the lesson is and where it is going. For example, the teacher may say, "That completes our description of clouds; now we will examine weather fronts." Like the sequencing of instructional materials, this method keeps the student informed on what is coming next so they will move to the next activity with little or no break in concentration.

Therefore, effective teachers manage transitions from one activity to another in a systematic way through efficient management of instructional matter, sequencing of instructional activities, moving students in groups, and employing academic transition signals. Through an efficient use of class time, achievement is increased because students spend more class time engaged in on-task behavior.

Successful transitions are achieved by using proactive strategies. Early in the year, the teacher pinpoints the transition periods in the day and anticipates possible behavior problems, such as students habitually returning late from lunch, or an autistic student having difficulty with change. After identifying possible problems with the environment or the schedule, the teacher plans proactive strategies to minimize or eliminate those problems. Proactive planning also gives the teacher the advantage of being prepared, addressing behaviors before they become problems, and incorporating strategies into the classroom management plan right away. Transition plans can be developed for each type of transition and the expected behaviors for each situation taught directly to the students.

SKILL 2.6 Understanding how to manage student behavior

Managing student behavior entails developing a management plan, which takes a proactive approach—that is, deciding what behaviors will be expected of the class as a whole, anticipating possible problems, and teaching the behaviors early in the school year. When students with disabilities are involved, the teacher should consider the impact each child's disability may have on behavior and possible problems that might arise; the teacher should be proactive in planning to prevent them.

For example, if a teacher knows that a student has ADHD and his IEP calls for alternate positions for working (e.g., standing, lying down, movement), the teacher should take this into consideration when setting up the classroom and when designing the behavior management plan.

Behavior management techniques should focus on positive procedures that can be used at home as well as at school. Involving the students (including those with disabilities) in the development of the classroom rules lets the students know the rationale for the rules and allows them to assume responsibility for them. Once the rules are established, enforcement and reinforcement for following the rules should begin immediately, and should be consistent.

Consequences, both positive and negative, should be introduced when the rules are introduced; they should be clearly stated and understood by all of the students. The nature of the consequence should match the nature of the behavior in question. For example, free time activities are good rewards for students who work hard and finish their work on time. Removal from a group and "time out" is a reasonable negative consequence for a student who is misbehaving in a way that disturbs others. The teacher must apply the consequence consistently and fairly, so the students will know what to expect.

About four to six classroom rules should be posted where students can easily see and read them. These rules should be stated positively and describe specific behaviors, so they are easy to understand. Certain rules may also be tailored to meet target goals and IEP requirements of individual students.

As the students demonstrate the behaviors, the teacher should provide reinforcement and corrective feedback. Periodic "refresher" practice can be done as needed; for example, it can be done after a long holiday or if students begin to "slack off." A copy of the classroom plan should be readily available for substitute use, and the classroom aide should also be familiar with the plan and procedures.

Behavior management techniques should focus on positive procedures that can be used at home as well as at school.

As the students demonstrate the behaviors, the teacher should provide reinforcement and corrective feedback.

The teacher should clarify and model the expected behavior for the students. In addition to the classroom management plan, a management plan should be developed for special situations, (e.g., fire drills) and transitions (e.g., going to and from the cafeteria). Periodic review of the rules, modeling of rules, and practice may be conducted as needed.

> The teacher should clarify and model the expected behavior for the students.

SKILL 2.7 Theory and practice of effective classroom management

Treatment models for learning disabilities have evolved in response to theories about their causes. The medical approach of the 1940s and 1950s used instructional practices such as study carrels; movement breaks from seated tasks; structured tasks and schedules corresponding with attention span; reduced noise and distractions; modifying tasks to fit functioning levels; and recorded lessons.

During the 1960s, the psychological processing approach advocated identifying student learning styles, using oral administration of tests and books on tape where auditory learning was preferred. It also advocated activities like reproduction of designs, use of simplified, uncluttered worksheets, attention to detail, discrimination of sounds and symbols, interviews, puppetry, role playing, and referential communication.

The instructional practices of the behavioral approach of the 1970s included task analysis; mastery of prerequisite skills; small, sequential learning steps; identification of functioning abilities; use of concrete, hands-on materials; use of oral and written materials simultaneously; use of visual, auditory, and tactile teaching aids; use of compensatory and supportive aids; error analysis; use of color; use of high-interest, low-vocabulary reading materials; and teacher-made or adapted instructional materials.

In the 1980s and 1990s, strategy approaches were postulated. The instructional strategies included giving clues to identify important information; encouraging "talking through" problems; setting up homework organizers; teaching how to take notes and organize content read; asking for periodic status reports on long-term assignments; teaching test-taking and study skills; use of mnemonic cues; use of index cards for review; and instruction in use of the calculator, tape recorder, and word processor.

At the present time, practices from each of these models are in evidence in special education settings. Most teachers utilize an eclectic approach. The contemporary practice emphasizes cognitive learning strategies in which we teach students how to learn, how to manage their own behaviors in school, and how to generalize information from one setting to another, as the ultimate goal is to produce self-sufficient, independent learners with skills to last a lifetime.

Assertive Discipline

Assertive discipline, developed by Canter and Canter, is an approach to classroom control that allows the teacher to constructively deal with misbehavior and maintain a supportive environment for the students. The following are the assumptions behind assertive discipline:

- Behavior is a choice

- Consequences for not following rules are natural and logical, not a series of threats or punishments

- Positive reinforcement occurs for desired behavior

- The focus is on the behavior and the situation, not the student's character

The assertive discipline plan should be developed as soon as the teacher meets the students. The students can become involved in developing and discussing the needs for the rules. Rules should be limited to four to six basic classroom rules that are simple to remember and positively stated (e.g., "Raise hand to speak" instead of "Don't talk without permission").

Recognize and remove roadblocks to assertive discipline

Replace negative expectations with positives and set reasonable limits for students. When dealing with students with certain disabilities, it is particularly important to plan ahead and make classroom modifications that will help the student be successful in following rules. Many students with learning or emotional disabilities have so much experience "failing" to measure up that they have given up trying to please teachers and parents. It may be necessary to "rig" the situation to ensure the student can experience success at first.

Practice an assertive response style

Clearly state teacher expectations and expect the students to comply with them.

Set limits

Take into consideration the students' behavioral needs and the teacher's expectations, and set limits for behavior. Decide what you will do when the rules are broken or followed.

Follow through promptly with consequences when students break the rules

The students should clearly know in advance what to expect when a rule is broken. Conversely, follow through with the promised rewards for compliance and good behavior. This reinforces the concept that individuals choose their behavior and that there are consequences for their behavior.

Devise a system of positive consequences

Positive consequences do not always have to be food or treats. However, rewards should not be promised if it is not possible to deliver them. The result is a more positive classroom.

Nonaversive Techniques

Token economy

Token economy is a system in which individuals receive tokens as a reward for a desired behavior. The tokens are collected and traded for an item or activity. In some cases the token is money, in others it might be stars on a chart. When the person earns enough money (or stars) he or she can buy a certain item or pay to participate in a desirable activity. This technique gives individuals a concrete motivator to perform the targeted behavior.

> *Example: The student is required to stay at his or her seat and work independently while the teacher works with someone else. Each time the student does this successfully, a sticker is put on a chart that, when filled, can be traded for a prize of some sort.*

Planned ignoring

Planned ignoring means the teacher determines that an inappropriate behavior will be ignored. This often works with attention-seeking behaviors. In the ideal situation, once the attention is removed the behavior ceases. It is important, however, to ensure that the student has other more appropriate behavioral options for getting the needed attention available, and that the teacher notices them, too.

> *Example: A student complains that he doesn't want to do a task, folds his arms, and turns away angrily and mutters. The teacher ignores the student and focuses on the students doing their work. The student eventually gets tired of being ignored, stops muttering, and gets to work (and the teacher pays attention to him!).*

Proximity control

An adult's close proximity to a student can often reduce or prevent undesirable behaviors.

> *Example: The rule is no talking. Jack turns to talk to Johnny. The teacher walks by and he stops talking. Sometimes the teacher can use a prearranged signal, such as tapping a book, so the student knows she is watching and will return to work.*

Self-assessment

Self-assessment is when the students are responsible for taking part in their own behavior management. The individual may be trained to self-record data. Typically someone may also collect data about the recorder's behavior or observe data recording sessions. Then the results are discussed and the person is rewarded for desirable behaviors. This strategy should be used only with mature individuals.

> *Example: A student constantly rushes through assignments and receives poor grades. The student is given a questionnaire to answer before turning in a paper. The questionnaire contained the following questions:*
>
> *Did I put the correct punctuation on all sentences?*
>
> *Have I capitalized the correct letters?*
>
> *Have I spaced between words?*
>
> *Did I thoroughly discuss the topic?*
>
> *Did I read the paper at least three times to look for errors?*
>
> *If the student answers yes to all the questions, and it looks like he or she actually did this, he or she would receive a good grade as an incentive to continue self-assessment.*

SKILL 2.8 Design and maintenance of a safe and supportive classroom environment that promotes student achievement

Physical Environment (Spatial Arrangements)

The physical setting of the classroom contributes a great deal to the propensity for students to learn. An adequate, well-built, and well-equipped classroom will invite students to learn. This has been called "invitational learning." This is even more important when students with disabilities are involved. Among the important factors to consider in the physical setting of the classroom are the following:

- Adequate physical space: A classroom must have adequate physical space so students can conduct themselves comfortably. Some students are distracted by windows, pencil sharpeners, doors, etc. Some students prefer the front, middle, or back rows. The needs of students with disabilities may be critical here. Wheelchairs need space to get around. Blind students need furniture to remain in fixed locations, etc.

- **Repair status:** The teacher has the responsibility to report any incidents of classroom disrepair to maintenance staff. Broken windows, falling plaster, exposed sharp surfaces, leaks in ceiling or walls, and other items of disrepair present hazards to students.

- **Lighting adequacy:** Another factor that must be considered is adequate lighting. Report any inadequacies in classroom illumination. Some students may require full-spectrum lighting due to a visual impairment. If these lights are necessary, reporting their failure as soon as possible will enable that student to have continuity in the learning environment.

- **Adequate entry/exit access:** Local fire and safety codes dictate entry and exit standards. In addition, all corridors and classrooms should be wheelchair accessible for students and others who use them. Older schools may not have this accessibility.

- **Ventilation/climate control:** Another consideration is adequate ventilation and climate control. Some classrooms in some states use air conditioning extensively. When a classroom is too cold, it is considered a distraction. Specialty classes (such as science) require specialized hoods for ventilation. Physical Education classes have the added responsibility for shower areas and specialized environments that must be heated, such as pool or athletic training rooms.

- **Coloration:** Classrooms with warmer, subdued colors contribute to students' concentration on tasks. Neutral colors for walls, ceiling, and carpet or tile are generally used in classrooms, so distraction due to classroom coloration is minimized.

In the modern classroom, there is a great deal of furniture, equipment, supplies, appliances, and learning aids to help the teacher teach and students learn. The classroom should be provided with furnishings that fit the purpose of the classroom. The kindergarten classroom may have a reading center, a playhouse, a puzzle table, student work desks/tables, a sandbox, and any other relevant learning/interest areas.

Whatever the arrangement of furniture and equipment may be, the teacher must provide for adequate traffic flow. Rows of desks must have adequate space between them for students to move and for the teacher to circulate. All areas must be open to line-of-sight supervision by the teacher.

In all cases, proper care must be taken to ensure student safety. Furniture and equipment should be situated safely at all times. No equipment, materials, boxes, etc., should be placed where they are in danger of falling over. Doors must have entry and exit accessibility at all times.

Noise level should also be considered as part of the physical environment. Students vary in the degree of quiet that they need and the amount of background noise or talking that they can tolerate without getting distracted or frustrated. Thus, a teacher must maintain an environment that is conducive to the learning of each child.

Instructional Arrangements

Instructional arrangements can also affect the degree to which students feel accepted. Learning styles refer to the ways in which individuals learn best. Physical settings, instructional arrangements, available materials, techniques, and individual preferences are all factors in the teacher's choice of instructional strategies. Information about the students' preferences can be gathered through a direct interview or a Likert-style checklist on which the student rates his or her preferences. By taking a student's instructional preferences into account, the teacher shows an acceptance of those preferences as legitimate and of value.

Some students work well in large groups; others prefer small groups or one-to-one instruction with the teacher, aide, or volunteer. Instructional arrangements also involve peer-tutoring situations with the student as tutor or tutee. The teacher also needs to consider how well the student works independently with seatwork. If the student is able to work in a manner that "feels right" to him or her, the student will feel like an accepted, valued member of the class.

See Skill 2.5: Organizing the learning environment, for further information.

DOMAIN III
INSTRUCTION

PERSONALIZED STUDY PLAN

KNOWN MATERIAL/ SKIP IT

PAGE	SKILL		
57	3.1:	Instructional strategies/techniques that are appropriate, considering students' ages and abilities	☐
	3.2:	Instructional strategies for ensuring individual academic success in one-to-one, small group, and large group settings	☐
	3.3:	Instructional strategies that facilitate maintenance and generalization of concepts	☐
	3.4:	Selection and implementation of research-based interventions for individual students	☐
	3.5:	Selection and implementation of supplementary and/ or functional curriculum	☐
	3.6:	Options for assistive technology	☐
	3.7:	Instructional strategies/techniques that support transition goals	☐
	3.8:	Preventive strategies and intervention strategies for at-risk learners	☐

SKILL 3.1 Instructional strategies/techniques that are appropriate, considering students' ages and abilities

The **IFSP** (for children birth to age three) and the **IEP** (for school age children, age three to twenty-one) are both mandated by the IDEA. They are legal documents meant to summarize relevant assessments and diagnoses, determine needed services, and provide a structure for the implementation of those services.

The IFSP focuses on a child's family as a whole in the context of daily life and preparation for school. It is designed for children who are diagnosed with a disability or a developmental delay or who are determined to be "at risk" for a delay or disability. The plan is developed when someone close to the child (parent, doctor, social worker, etc.) brings their concerns to the state health department and a team of specialists, parents, and family members meets to evaluate the child's needs.

The IFSP usually includes statements of the child's levels of cognitive, language, communication, physical, and emotional functioning, as well as diagnoses of any specific problems. The plan also lists needed services and methods by which these services will be delivered. The IFSP often leads to IEP development when the child enters school.

An IEP is the document that forms the basis for special services and instruction in the educational setting. An IEP is developed when someone (e.g., parent, teacher, specialist) asks for a meeting to consider the child's needs. Typical "team" members at a meeting include parents (and sometimes parent advocates), a general education teacher familiar with state standards, any special education teachers involved, specialists who can test or interpret tests for the team, and a representative of the school district. The child may also be present, especially in secondary education.

If the team determines that the child is eligible for special education services, an IEP is written. According to IDEA, each IEP must contain the following:

- A statement of the present levels of educational performance of the child

- A statement of annual goals, including short-term instructional objectives

- A statement of the specific educational services to be provided to the child, and the extent to which the child will be able to participate in regular educational programs

- The projected date for initiation and anticipated duration of such services

- Appropriate objective criteria and evaluation procedures and schedules for determining, on at least an annual basis, whether instructional objectives are being achieved

IFSP (INDIVIDUALIZED FAMILY SERVICE PLAN): an IDEA-mandated legal document meant to summarize relevant assessments and diagnoses, determine needed services, and provide a structure for the implementation of those services for children from birth to age three

IEP (INDIVIDUALIZED EDUCATION PLAN): an IDEA-mandated legal document meant to summarize relevant assessments and diagnoses, determine needed services, and provide a structure for the implementation of those services for school-age children aged three to twenty-one

- Instructional and program accommodations and supports that must be provided throughout the educational settings and, specifically, in state- and district-mandated testing

- A clear rationale for any placement that involves nonparticipation in any part of the general education classroom

- Transition services, as appropriate and needed

All teachers and staff who interact with a child on an IEP are required to follow the dictates of the IEP. In addition to goals and objectives, the IEP will specify what accommodations or instructional modifications are to be provided to the child. Accommodations usually concern access to the curriculum. A child with accommodations to access the curriculum will follow the same grade level standards and goals as general education students and be graded on the same scale. Modifications usually refer to changes that significantly alter the standards, content, instructional level, or performance level required of the student. This means the student will be graded differently from grade peers. Whatever terminology is used, these distinctions are important, and it is the teacher's responsibility to be familiar with all aspects of the IEP, so as to ensure compliance with it.

As a special needs educator, it is imperative to look to the general education curriculum to develop appropriate goals and objectives for Individual Education Plans (IEPs). Since many students with disabilities are unable to complete the general education curriculum at the same level and at the same pace as students without disabilities, it is necessary to develop appropriate strategies and skills to prioritize the curriculum areas into attainable goals and objectives for these students.

> *Since many students with disabilities are unable to complete the general education curriculum at the same level and at the same pace as students without disabilities, it is necessary to develop appropriate strategies and skills to prioritize the curriculum areas into attainable goals and objectives for these students.*

The first step in prioritizing curriculum areas is to look for high-stakes areas or those areas that are most easily generalized to others. In this way, the teacher can target these skills with the students and provide the most intense instruction possible in the shortest amount of time. Choosing these types of skills provides the necessary fundamental knowledge students need to be successful. There is always more to learn, but providing students with a solid foundation allows them the opportunity to achieve success in the future.

Once the curriculum has been prioritized into meaningful areas, a gradation of success can be planned. In this way, students can tackle the skills in smaller, more manageable chunks of information in order to ensure mastery and success. It is necessary to analyze long-term goals and break them down into steps, beginning with entry-level objectives and working up to the final goal of mastery. Taking the time to build by smaller steps, even if the students are only on those steps for short periods of time, provides a more realistic path. These paths may be measured in weeks, months, or even years, depending on the abilities of the students, but should always be moving forward toward the end goal of mastery of a specific objective.

The teacher and team must be very skilled at writing academic objectives that fall within the guidelines of the state and local expectations. In addition, these objectives must be measurable so that, when the unit or semester is complete, he or she can know for sure whether or not goals have been met. Once long-range goals have been identified and established, the team must ensure that all goals and objectives are in conjunction with student abilities and needs.

Assessments are discussed further in Skill 4.2. Sometimes, the curriculum itself is not the issue, but, rather, the manner in which the curriculum is taught. Modification and adaptation of the regular education curriculum and instruction is one of the cornerstones of special education services; it needs to be considered an integral part of this process. When prioritizing and planning appropriate instruction for goals and objectives, it is imperative to keep in mind which areas can be taught with simple modifications or adaptations and still yield student success. This balancing act is ongoing throughout special education.

> *The teacher and team must be very skilled at writing academic objectives that fall within the guidelines of the state and local expectations.*

SKILL 3.2 Instructional strategies for ensuring individual academic success in one-to-one, small group, and large group settings

Adapting the Overall Instructional Environment

The teacher can modify the classroom instructional environment in several ways.

Individual student variables

Some students with disabilities benefit from sitting close to the teacher or away from windows. Others (with ADHD, for example) might benefit from wiggle seats or fiddle objects, still others from an FM system or cubicles that reduce distractions. Seating that reduces distractions serves also to reduce the cognitive load of lessons by removing the need for the students to block distractions themselves.

Classroom organization

Many students with learning disabilities benefit from a highly structured environment in which physical areas (e.g., supplies, reading, math, writing) are clearly labeled and a schedule for the day prominently displayed. Individual schedule charts can be useful if some students follow different schedules, such as leaving periodically for a resource room or specialized therapy. Such schedules reduce the cognitive load required to simply get through the day and provide increased context for the student navigating the daily routine.

The teacher can also vary grouping arrangements (e.g., large group, small group, peer tutoring, or learning centers) with student needs in mind. Five basic types of grouping arrangements are typically used in the classroom, outlined in the following paragraphs.

Large group with teacher

Examples of appropriate activities include show and tell, discussions, watching plays or movies, brainstorming ideas, and playing games. In general education classrooms, science, social studies, and most content area subjects are taught in large groups. The advantage of large-group instruction is that it is time-efficient and prepares students for higher levels of secondary and postsecondary education settings. However, with large groups, instruction cannot be as easily differentiated or tailored to individual student needs or learning styles. Mercer and Mercer (1985) recommend the following guidelines for effective large-group instruction:

- Keep instruction short, ranging from five to fifteen minutes for first grade to seventh grade; five to forty minutes for grades eight to twelve

- Use questions to involve all students, use lecture-pause routines, and encourage active participation among the lower-performing students

- Incorporate visual aids to promote understanding and maintain a lively pace

- Break up the presentation with different rates of speaking, giving students a "stretch break," varying voice volume, etc.

- Establish rules of conduct for large groups and praise students who follow the rules

When students with special needs are included in large group instruction, care must be taken to conduct the activity with their needs in mind. For example, if a particular student may have a limited recall or understanding of a subject, it can be useful to ask the student a concrete question or let the student answer before anyone else so his or her answer is not "taken" by someone else. Choral responses regarding key points can help provide context and support for students with some disabilities, as well.

Small group instruction

Small group instruction usually includes five to seven students and is recommended for teaching basic academic skills such as math facts or reading, and for introducing many abstract content area concepts. This model is especially effective for students with learning problems. Composition of the groups should be flexible to accommodate different rates of progress through instruction. Some of the advantages of teaching in small groups are that the teacher is better able to tailor the instruction to the special needs of certain students, provide feedback, monitor student progress, and give more individual attention and praise. With small groups, the teacher must provide a steady pace for the lesson, provide questions and activities that allow all to participate, and include lots of praise. Small groups can also make differentiated instruction easier and more practical.

One student with teacher

One-to-one tutorial teaching can be used to provide extra assistance to individual students. Such tutoring may be scheduled at set times during the day or provided as the need arises. The tutoring model is typically found more often in elementary and resource classrooms than in secondary settings and is particularly effective for students with certain disabilities.

Peer tutoring

In an effective peer tutoring arrangement, the teacher trains the peer tutors and matches them with students who need extra practice and assistance. In addition to academic skills, the arrangement can help both students work on social skills such as cooperation and self-esteem. Both students may be working on the same material or the tutee may be working to strengthen areas of weakness. The teacher determines the target goals, selects the material, sets up the guidelines, trains the student tutors in the rules and methods of the sessions, and monitors and evaluates the sessions. Care must be taken, however, to avoid the appearance that some students are smarter than others and that the "smarter" students have more work because of the "slower" students. It can be very helpful if the teacher can find something that allows the tutee in one situation to act as tutor in another.

Cooperative learning

Cooperative learning differs from peer tutoring in that students are grouped in teams or small groups and the methods are based on teamwork, individual accountability, and team reward. Individual students are responsible for their own learning and share of the work as well as the group's success. As with peer tutoring, the goals, target skills, materials, and guidelines are developed by the teacher. Teamwork skills may also need to be taught. By focusing on team goals, all members of the team are encouraged to help each other as well as improve their individual performance. When students with disabilities are included in such cooperative teams, it is imperative that the teacher arrange the tasks so that there is something substantive and important for each member of the group to contribute.

SKILL 3.3 Instructional strategies that facilitate maintenance and generalization of concepts

Application of skills to a variety of real-world contexts requires that students generalize or transfer those skills from the setting in which they are learned to a different setting in which they will be used (e.g., daily home life and work). This generalization will be far more likely to occur if the instructional setting mirrors the home/job setting. Although specific settings and techniques will vary depending upon the individual student's needs, skills learned and practiced in a setting as close to the real-world setting as possible will be more likely to transfer to that real-world setting.

Think about mathematics for a moment: applying principles of generalization specifically to math, the following practices can help students learn to use their math skills in real-world contexts. Use varied real-world problems in teaching to deepen application of learned skills. Once a computational or problem-solving skill has been studied, design real-world problems that need to be solved using it. For example, use grocery store flyers for a variety of exercises in both computation and problem solving.

Use consistency in initial teaching situations, and later introduce variety in format, procedure, and use of examples. Have the same information presented by different teachers, in different settings, and under varying conditions. This requires good collaboration among various teachers and professionals, but it will be helpful if all the teachers working with the student are aware of what is currently being taught in the classroom.

Teach students to actively look for ways a particular skill might be used.

Teach students to actively look for ways a particular skill might be used and record instances of this generalization. Cooperative learning can be used here: for example, assign a small group to brainstorm ways to use the four basic math operations in the grocery store or on the baseball field.

Associate naturally occurring stimuli when possible (e.g., the above use of grocery flyers). Arranging for practice in the real-life setting can greatly enhance generalization (e.g., a field trip to the grocery store).

Real-world applications offer highly motivating opportunities for practice. This promotes the development of generalization and often motivates learners, since they can often understand the validity of the lesson when it is applied to realistic situations.

SKILL 3.4 Selection and implementation of research-based interventions for individual students

When choosing an approach or technique, teachers need to keep in mind that they are accountable for teaching subjects using varied, *research-based approaches with measurable outcomes*. Therefore, whatever approach a teacher chooses should take into account current research on effective teaching methods. Research-based interventions in both reading and math are delineated below.

Research on Critical Components of Reading Development

In 2000, the National Reading Panel released its now well-known report on teaching children to read. This report side-stepped the debate between phonics and whole-language approaches and argued, essentially, that both letter-sound recognition and comprehension of the text are important to successful reading. It identified five critical areas of reading instruction:

1. **PHONEMIC AWARENESS:** The understanding that spoken words are made up of a sequence of individual sounds or phonemes. This is just one part of overall **PHONOLOGICAL AWARENESS**, the awareness of such aspects of spoken language as words as units, syllables within words, sentences, etc.

2. **PHONICS:** The process of linking sounds to letter symbols and combining them to make words

3. **FLUENCY:** The ability to read with speed, accuracy, and proper expression without conscious attention, and to handle both word recognition and comprehension simultaneously

4. **VOCABULARY:** The part of comprehension based on the meaning of individual words in context

5. **COMPREHENSION:** The process of getting meaning or information from text, which occurs on multiple levels, from literal to abstract

Methods used to teach these skills are often featured in a balanced literacy curriculum that focuses on the use of skills in various instructional contexts. For example, a phonics component tailored to individual student needs is included; for independent reading, students choose books at their reading levels that interest them; with guided reading, teachers work with small groups of students to help them with their particular reading problems; with whole group reading, the entire class will read the same text and the teacher will incorporate activities to help students learn phonics, comprehension, fluency, and vocabulary.

PHONEMIC AWARENESS: the understanding that spoken words are made up of a sequence of individual sounds or phonemes

PHONOLOGICAL AWARENESS: the awareness of such aspects of spoken language as words as units, syllables within words, sentences, etc.

PHONICS: the process of linking sounds to letter symbols and combining them to make words

FLUENCY: the ability to read with speed, accuracy, and proper expression without conscious attention, and to handle both word recognition and comprehension simultaneously

VOCABULARY: the part of comprehension based on the meaning of individual words in context

COMPREHENSION: the process of getting meaning or information from text, which occurs on multiple levels, from literal to abstract

Developmental reading programs emphasize daily, sequential instruction. Instructional materials usually feature a series of books as the core of the program.

Phonics approach

With this approach, word recognition is taught through grapheme-phoneme associations, with the goal of teaching the student to independently apply these skills to new words.

In a variation of a straight phonics program, an onset-rhyme or whole-word approach is used. This means that words are taught in word families (e.g., cat, hat, pat, and rat). The focus is on words that can be blended instead of isolated sounds. Words are chosen on the basis of similar spelling patterns, and irregular spelling words are taught as sight words. The consistent visual patterns of the lessons guide students from familiar words to less familiar words to irregular words.

Whole-language approach

Through the whole-language approach, reading is taught as a holistic, meaning-oriented activity and is not broken down into a collection of skills. This approach relies heavily on literature or trade books selected for a particular purpose. Reading is taught as part of a total language-arts program, and the curriculum seeks to develop instruction in real problems and ideas. Phonics is not taught in a structured, systematic way. Students are assumed to develop their phonetic awareness through exposure to print. Writing is taught as a complement to reading. Though the integration of reading with writing is an advantage of the whole-language approach, the approach has been criticized for the lack of direct instruction in specific skill strategies.

Language-experience approach

The language-experience approach is similar to the whole-language approach in that reading is considered a personal act, literature is emphasized, and students are encouraged to write about their own life experiences. Principles of this approach include:

- What students think about, they can talk about
- What students say, they can write or dictate
- What students write or dictate, they can read. (It should be noted, however, that this is often not true for students with disabilities such as Dyslexia. Many students with disabilities can dictate an excellent composition, but when they write it down, they cannot read it back.)

Although the emphasis on student experience and creativity stimulates interest and motivation, and can be beneficial in the composition portion, this method shares the disadvantages of the whole-language method, specifically the absence of a phonics component. Teachers would need to add this missing component into the program in some way. In addition, there is no set method of evaluating student progress.

Individualized-reading approach

Students select their own reading materials according to interest and ability with this approach, and progress at their own individual rates. Word recognition and comprehension are taught as the student needs them. The teacher's role is to diagnose errors and prescribe materials, although the final choice is made by the students. Individual work may be supplemented by group activities with basal readers and workbooks for specific reading skills. The lack of systematic checks and developmental skills and emphasis on self-learning may be a disadvantage for students with learning problems. However, such an approach can be integrated into almost any more global reading program and can be used to enhance student reading independence and enjoyment.

Research and Overview of Principles of Math Instruction

Based on the child's development, Baratta-Lorton (1978) described three levels of instruction necessary to help a child move through any mathematics curriculum. Modern research has consistently confirmed this approach to teaching math.

1. Concept Level: At this level, the child needs *repeated and varied* inter-action with manipulatives. The child needs to interact intensively with a variety of objects, to see patterns, combinations, and relationships among the objects before he or she can internalize concepts. When introducing any new concept, this is the level at which the child will spend the most time. It is important to remember that the objects are not being used by the teacher to demonstrate concepts, but by the child to *discover* concepts and relationships. The teacher's role is to ask questions that trigger higher-order thinking and learning from the child.

2. Connecting Level: At this level, the child learns to assign symbols or representations to the objects and the operations carried out on the objects. However, the objects or manipulatives are still very present and remain part of the process. Labeling the objects and operations with symbols in the presence of the objects or manipulatives serves as a connection from the concrete level to the next level. The child can move on from this level more quickly and whenever ready to do so.

3. Symbolic Level: At this level, the child can use symbols without manipulatives. The child understands the abstract concepts behind the symbols and can operate on and with symbols alone.

The National Council of Teachers of Mathematics (NCTM)'s 2000 outline of principles upon which mathematics instruction should be based provides a similar process by which math concepts should be taught. This document states that instruction and exploration should go through three stages of *representation* (the procedure for modeling and interpreting organization of objects and mathematical operations):

CONCRETE REPRESENTATIONS: the extensive exploration and use of objects and manipulatives to discover and then demonstrate operations and relationships

1. **CONCRETE REPRESENTATIONS:** The extensive exploration and use of objects and manipulatives to discover and then demonstrate operations and relationships

PICTORIAL REPRESENTATIONS: the use of concrete pictures of objects and actions, often in the presence of the objects, as discoveries and demonstrations are made

2. **PICTORIAL REPRESENTATIONS** (semi-abstract): The use of concrete pictures of objects and actions, often in the presence of the objects, as discoveries and demonstrations are made

SYMBOLIC REPRESENTATIONS: the use of symbols exclusively to conduct operations, explorations and discoveries about math concepts

3. **SYMBOLIC REPRESENTATIONS** (abstract): The use of symbols exclusively to conduct operations, explorations, and discoveries about math concepts

The NCTM report goes on to describe a mathematics program based on NCTM standards and current research as having the following general characteristics:

- Children will be actively engaged in exploring math concepts and doing math. There will be hands-on, concrete exploration, as well talking about, reading about, and writing about math.

- Students will be encouraged to "stretch" their math sense and "think like mathematicians." High standards will be expected, but the learning setting will be safe enough for children to take risks and make mistakes in order to learn and enjoy learning.

- Teachers will ask stimulating questions that encourage children to make new discoveries and connections, and to reveal concepts they already know.

- Cooperative learning will take place. Children will learn from talking to one another about math and through working together.

- Math will be part of the "real world" and connections to that real world will be made for all activities and concepts.

- Content taught will cover a wide range of topics and applications, not only computation, but the concepts behind computation and use and the math language to discuss these connections.

A review of research by David Allsopp (in Allsopp, Kyger, & Lovin, 2007) suggests additional general practices:

- Teaching problem-solving strategies is more effective than exclusively using rote practice.

- Concrete instruction, persistently applied throughout the levels of the mathematics curriculum, is effective in helping students develop computation and problem-solving skills and to prepare for abstract mathematics work.

- Ongoing assessment of students' performance, as well as sharing and discussing their progress and successes with them, improves learning outcomes.

- Engaging students as active participants in their learning by encouraging and teaching metacognitive behaviors like goal-setting, self-monitoring, and self-talk boosts math proficiency and boosts performance. The same outcome is true for showing them how to apply these skills not only to their mathematics work but also to general problem solving.

- Well-planned cooperative learning activities, such as peer tutoring and work groups, can offer students opportunities for meaningful practice and skill enhancement.

Developing Problem-Solving Skills

Developing critical-thinking and problem-solving skills in mathematics goes beyond simply solving "word problems" in a math textbook. **PROBLEM SOLVING** is the process of applying previously-acquired knowledge to new and novel situations, and it involves more than simply reading word problems, deciding on correct conceptual procedures, and performing the computations. It involves posing questions; analyzing situations; hypothesizing, translating, and illustrating results; drawing diagrams; using trial and error; and *explaining* results.

> **PROBLEM SOLVING:** the process of applying previously-acquired knowledge to new and novel situations

Children will need to learn a variety of problem-solving strategies to keep in their personal "tool kit" for solving mathematical problems in school and in everyday life. Some of these strategies include:

- Acting out the problem or using manipulatives

- Drawing pictures, graphs, or tables

- Identifying simpler problems with similar solutions

- Guessing and checking possible solutions

- Using a flow chart to outline the problem or the steps in it

- Constructing 3D models

- Looking for patterns

- Working backward

- Developing their own idiosyncratic strategies

Students must also learn the *process* of problem solving, and this requires a different type of instruction. Some research-based techniques to help children become active, confident problem solvers, regardless of the level or type of problem, include:

- Address problem solving outside of math and help students learn how to transfer what they learn to math. For example, find time in the day to present small problems to the class and spend time soliciting ideas on how to solve the problems. Teachers can use such things as fables and folktales as starting points without including the solution (e.g., tell about the crow and the water pitcher but don't tell what the crow did to get the water; let the students figure something out). Shannon (1994) presents a variety of folktales that can be used as problem-solving starters.

- Let students attempt their individual ways of solving, rather than prescribing a particular way as correct. While many math problems have only one correct answer, many have more than one correct answer (e.g., "Which of these toys could Tom buy with his $10?" might have more than one answer, and many higher math problems require a range of answers). In addition, there may be a number of ways to arrive at a correct answer.

- *Discuss* each child's method and highlight the multiple ways to solve a problem (e.g., "Ok, you added, Tom drew a picture, let's see what Sue did.").

- Use cooperative learning groups; assign a problem and let children work together. A variation of a common procedure used in reading can be very useful here: assign each student a "job" (e.g., one looks for vocabulary terms critical to solution, one looks for numbers and amounts, one looks for operations, one decides relevant vs. irrelevant information, one does computation, etc).

SKILL 3.5 Selection and implementation of supplementary and/or functional curriculum

In order for students to apply critical thinking and problem-solving skills learned in school to decisions relevant to functional life needs, students must be able to *generalize* or *transfer* these skills from the school setting to the functional living setting of home life, jobs, and leisure. Generalization training is a procedure in which a behavior is reinforced in each of a series of situations (see Skill 3.3) until the student begins to apply the learned behavior to new situations more automatically. The more similar two situations are, the easier it is for the student to transfer learned behavior to the new situation.

This is particularly true of functional skills involved in independent living and the workplace. Skills learned in the school setting are far more likely to generalize to home life or the workplace if the school setting resembles the home or work setting.

Even when the settings are deliberately made as similar as possible, however, many students with disabilities will need instruction specifically designed to help them think about how to apply what they have learned in school to real-life problems. These are higher-order or critical-thinking skills because they require students to *think about thinking*. For example, these skills can be found in:

- Balancing a checkbook and analyzing bills for overcharges

- Comparing shopping ads or catalogue deals

- Following news stories

- Reading a TV guide and planning for recording programs

- Gathering information/data from diverse sources to plan a project

- Following a sequence of directions in a recipe or on the job

- Looking for cause and effect relationships (e.g., why is the dog barking or the baby crying?)

- Appropriate responses and use of community resources (e.g., call the electrical company if the power is out, call the doctor and my work supervisor if I am sick)

- Evaluating information relevant to making a given decision (e.g., deciding which movie to go to might involve cost, time, duration, personal interest, and available transportation)

Both the math problem-solving strategies and the techniques for helping students to apply them to real life (discussed in Skill 3.4) can be adapted for use with many functional life skills. General techniques for improving the transfer of problem solving skills are as follows:

- Use of cooperative learning groups or whole class discussions of how to solve problems mentioned might involve common home life and job-related problems, rather than folktales or math. Role playing can be particularly effective in cooperative groups for this purpose.

- Allowing students or groups of students to try their own solutions and discussing various approaches that might work can help them learn there may be more than one solution to a problem. For example, if the proposed problem

> Skills learned in the school setting are far more likely to generalize to home life or the workplace if the school setting resembles the home or work setting.

is how to get to work on time, solutions might include walking (depending on the distance), biking, a bus route, subway, driving or carpooling, or even a taxi.

- Helping students identify similarities in functional problems might involve helping them see that getting to work on time and getting to a movie on time involve many of the same skills, etc.

For functional life problems, students can ask themselves:

- What is the problem or decision, or what do I want to do? (main idea)

- What do I need in order to do it? (information needed to solve)

- What do I need to find out that I don't already know? (relevant information)

- How can I find out what I need to know? (strategy or plan)

- Solve the problem or make a decision

- Check to see if decision or solution actually gets me what I wanted

Attention to learner needs during planning is essential. It includes identifying the things students already know or need to know; matching learner needs with instructional elements such as content, materials, activities, and goals; and determining whether or not students have performed at an acceptable level, following instruction.

The ability to create a personal chart of students' functional learning and emotional growth found within the performance-based assessment of individualized portfolios can be useful for both students and teachers. Teachers can use semester portfolios to gauge student progress and the personal growth of students who are constantly trying to apply their learning to new situations. When a student studies to master a functional skill and makes a visual of his or her learning, it can help connect the learning to a higher level of thinking that can be generalized to new situations that were not specifically studied in class.

SKILL 3.6 Options for assistive technology

IDEA provides the following definition of an ASSISTIVE TECHNOLOGY DEVICE:

"Any item, piece of equipment or product system, whether acquired commercially off the shelf, modified, or customized that is used to increase, maintain or improve functional capabilities of children with disabilities."

IDEA 2004 clarified that assistive technology "does not include a medical device that is surgically implanted, or the replacement of such device."

Almost anything can be considered assistive technology if it can be used to increase, maintain, or improve the functioning of a person with a disability.

Some areas in which assistive technology (AT) may be used:

- Communication
- Hearing
- Vision
- Environmental management
- Academic concepts related to reading, writing, or using numbers
- Body movement
- Leisure activities
- Memory
- Work or vocational skills

> **ASSISTIVE TECHNOLOGY DEVICE:** any item, piece of equipment or product system, whether acquired commercially off the shelf, modified, or customized that is used to increase, maintain or improve functional capabilities of children with disabilities

AT devices can increase the following for a person with a disability:

- Level of independence
- Quality of life
- Productivity
- Performance
- Educational/vocational options
- Success in regular education settings

A variety of AT devices are available to address the functional capabilities of students with disabilities. Zabala (2000) identified AT devices in fourteen major areas.

Academic and Learning Aids

Academic and learning aids are electronic and nonelectronic aids such as calculators, spell checkers, portable word processors, and computer-based software solutions that assist the student in academic areas.

Reading

AT solutions that address difficulty with reading may include:

- Colored overlays: Overlays that alter the contrast between the text and background are helpful for students with perceptual difficulties. It may be necessary to experiment to determine the best color or combination of colors for a student.

- Reading window: A simple, no-tech solution for students who have difficulty with tracking. A "frame" is constructed from tag board or cardboard, allowing the student to see one line of text at a time as he or she moves down the page.

- Spell checker or talking dictionary: Students type in words they are having difficulty reading and the device will say the word for them.

- **Auditory textbooks:** Students who have difficulty reading traditional print texts may use audio-taped texts or texts on CDs to follow along as the text is read aloud. Textbooks on tape or CD are available to students with disabilities through Recordings for the Blind and Dyslexic, as are specialized CD players that allow the student to key in pages, headings, or chapters to access specific text quickly. Some even allow the student to insert electronic bookmarks.

- **Talking word processing programs:** Low-cost software applications that provide speech output of text displayed on the computer monitor. Some programs highlight the text as it is read.

Spelling

AT is available to support spelling in handwritten and computer-generated text.

- **Personal word list or dictionary:** Students maintain a list of commonly misspelled words for personal reference; can be handwritten or computer-generated.

- **Hand-held spell checker:** Students type in words, and a list of correctly spelled words that closely approximate the misspelled word is provided. Some models offer speech feedback.

- **Word processing program with spell check:** Most word processing programs offer a spell check feature in which misspelled words are underlined.

- **Talking word processing program with spell check:** These programs are helpful for students who cannot visually identify the correct word on a traditional spell check program. The talking feature allows the student to "listen" for the correct spelling of the word.

Writing

AT to support writing includes a number of low- and high-tech options.

- **Alternative paper:** For students with fine motor difficulties, modifying the writing paper may be appropriate. One solution is to provide paper with bold lines. Another solution is to use a tactile paper that has a raised line that the student can actually feel. Some students benefit from using graph paper, placing one letter in each box, to improve legibility. Graph paper can also be used for math problems, to assure that the numbers are in alignment.

- **Pencil grips:** This is an inexpensive alternative that gives the student with fine motor difficulties a larger and more supportive means of grasping a pencil.

- **Adapted tape recorder:** Students who have difficulty with writing may be allowed to tape record some of their assignments. Adapted tape recorders can also be used to record class lectures for students who have difficulty taking notes. Tape recorders with an index feature allow the student to mark key points on a tape for later reference.

- **Portable word processor:** For students with significant writing difficulties, a portable word processor can provide an alternative to using pencil and paper. These devices use a full size keyboard and allow the student to type in text. Files can be stored in the device to be uploaded to a computer at a later time. Advantages over a traditional computer or laptop are the economical price, portability, and long battery life.

- **Talking word processor software:** These programs provide feedback by reading aloud what the student has typed in, allowing the student to hear what he has written. This type of multisensory feedback assists the student in identifying and correcting errors.

- **Word prediction software:** This type of software is beneficial for students who have difficulty with spelling and grammar. As the first letter or letters of a word are typed in, the computer predicts the word the student is typing. This type of technology is beneficial to students who type slowly, as it reduces the number of keystrokes needed to complete a word.

- **Outlining and webbing software:** This type of software assists students who have difficulty organizing thoughts and planning. Webbing programs allow for graphic diagrams to give the student a visual representation of what is needed to complete the writing task.

- **Voice recognition software:** This type of software has gained in popularity in recent years due to its wide commercial applications. Voice recognition allows the student to "speak" into the computer, and the spoken word is translated into written text on the computer screen.

Math

To support students with difficulties in math, both low-tech and high-tech options are available.

- **Calculators:** Students who have difficulty performing math calculations can benefit from the use of a calculator. Adapted calculators may have larger buttons or larger display screens that are useful for students with physical disabilities. Talking calculators are available for students with visual impairments.

- **On-screen electronic worksheets:** For student with physical disabilities who have difficulty with writing, worksheets can be produced in an on-screen format, allowing the student to use a computer screen to answer the questions.

- Manipulatives of all types: Students who have difficulty acquiring or retaining math concepts often benefit from objects designed to provide a kinesthetic or visual illustration of the concept. These low-tech aids include such things as place value blocks, fraction strips, geared clocks, play money, etc.

Aids for Daily Living

Devices to assist with self-help skills in activities such as eating, bathing, cooking, dressing, toileting, and home maintenance include:

- Adapted eating utensils: These are low-tech aides to assist students with feeding themselves. Adapted utensils may include forks, spoon, and knives with an enlarged handle to allow a better grasp or with straps or cuffs for attaching the utensils to the hand for stability. Electronic devices to assist with eating are also available for students with more severe physical disabilities.

- Adapted drinking aids: Adaptations to cups and glasses include modified handles or positioning aids to stabilize the cup on a table or wheelchair tray. Some drinking utensils may have tops or modified rims to prevent spillage.

- Self-care aids: Students may need assistance to complete self-care tasks such as dressing, grooming, and toileting. Dressing aids include items such as adapted sock aids for putting on and taking off socks, zipper grips for pulling zippers up and down, no-tie curly laces for shoes, and button hooks to assist in buttoning. Grooming aids include adapted handles on brushes, combs, and toothbrushes. Toileting aids could include adapted toilet seats and safety rails for transferring on and off the toilet.

Assistive Listening Devices and Environmental Aids

Assistive listening devices and environmental aids are electronic and nonelectronic aids such as amplification devices, closed captioning systems, and environmental alert systems that assist a student with a hearing impairment to access information that is typically presented through an auditory modality.

- Assistive listening devices: These devices amplify sound and speech and are appropriate for a student with a hearing impairment. Personal amplification systems are portable and can be used in different environments. These systems consist of a transmitter that transmits the sound to the student's receiving unit. Personal sound field systems consist of a transmitter and a receiver, along with a portable speaker. Sound field systems can also be installed in entire rooms.

- **Text telephones (TTY):** Students with hearing impairments may use the TTY keyboard to type messages over the telephone. Some TTYs have answering machines and some models offer a print-out of the text.

- **Closed captioning devices:** Modern televisions are equipped with closed captioning options that present the text on the television screen.

- **Environmental aids:** These can included adapted clocks, notification systems, pagers, and warning devices. Visual alert systems may be configured to alert the student of a doorbell, telephone ringing, or smoke detector sounding. Personal pagers may have vibrating and text messaging options.

- **Real-time captioning:** This may be used to caption speech, such as class lectures and presentations, to a text display. A computer with specialized software and a projection system are needed for this type of software.

Augmentative Communication

Augmentative communication consists of electronic and nonelectronic devices and software solutions that provide a means for expressive and receptive communication for students with speech and language impairments.

- **Object-based communication displays:** Low-tech solutions that use actual objects to represent daily activities. The student selects or touches the object to communicate a want or need.

- **Picture communication boards and books:** Low-tech solutions that use pictures to represent messages. The pictures are organized according to categories or activities in the student's day.

- **Alphabet boards:** Students who are able to spell but have limited language can use an alphabet board to communicate. The student touches the letters to spell out words, phrases, or sentences.

- **Talking switches:** These devices allow for recording of one or two messages. The student activates the switch to "say" the message. A picture may be used in conjunction with the device.

- **Voice output devices (low-tech):** Multiple messages can be recorded on these devices. Messages are recorded and accessed by the student to communicate wants and needs. The low-tech models can range in capacity from one to up to sixty-four messages. Pictures are used on the device as a representative of each message.

- **Voice output devices (middle-tech):** On these devices, the messages are represented by picture symbols. These devices have the capacity to store multiple messages on multiple levels.

- **Voice output devices (high-tech):** High-tech voice output devices are very sophisticated pieces of technology that allow the student to use a computer-generated voice to speak for him or her. Some devices uses paper-based displays, while others are computer-generated (dynamic) displays. Some offer a keyboard to allow the student to type in messages as well.

- **Integrated communication solutions:** Several software-based applications are available that use a laptop computer in conjunction with a voice output system.

Computer Access and Instruction

These are input and output devices, alternative access aids, modified or alternative keyboards, switches, special software, and other devices and software solutions that assist a student with a disability to use a computer.

- **Adaptive pointing devices:** Hand-held pointers, hand splints, and mouth sticks can assist the student with physical disabilities to access a computer without the use of hands.

- **Keyboard adaptations:** The computer keyboard can be adapted for students with physical disabilities. Keyguards are devices that cover the computer keyboard and allow access through holes that keep the student from hitting more than one key at a time.

- **Alternative keyboards:** Alternative keyboards may be enlarged for students who need larger targets, or they could be mini keyboards for students with limited movement.

- **Touch screens:** Touch screens allow access to the computer by touch, rather than by using the keyboard or mouse. This is another area of assistive technology that has shown a lot of growth in recent years, due to the wide commercial usage of touch screen products.

- **On-Screen keyboards:** For students who have difficulty using a traditional keyboard, an on-screen keyboard allows the student to write using a mouse, switch, or a scanning system.

- **Mouse alternatives:** Mouse alternatives include trackballs, joysticks, and track pads and are appropriate for students who have difficulty using a traditional mouse.

- **Adaptive output:** Text and graphics on the computer screen can be enlarged for students with visual impairments. Text displayed can also be read aloud by the use of screen reading applications. Printers that print Braille from text typed on the computer are also available for students with visual impairments.

Environmental Controls

Environmental controls are devices such as switches, environmental control units, and adapted appliances that are used by a student with a physical disability to increase independence. These devices allow the student to use alternate devices, such as switches to control items such as lights, televisions, and door locks.

Mobility Aids

Mobility aids are aids that increase personal mobility, such as wheelchairs, walkers, canes, crutches, and scooters.

Prevocational and Vocational Aids

Prevocational and vocational aids are aids and adaptations that are used to assist a student in completing prevocational and vocational tasks, such as picture-based task analysis sheets, adapted knobs, adapted timers, and adapted watches.

Recreation and Leisure Aids

Recreation and leisure aids are aids such as adapted books, switch-adapted toys, and leisure computer-based software applications that are used by a student with a disability to increase participation and independence in recreation and leisure activities.

- Game and puzzle adaptations: Games and puzzles may be adapted by the addition of knobs to the pieces, by using card holders, and by using grabbing devices to pick up the pieces.

- Book adaptations: Adaptations to books may include enlarging the text, providing an audio version to read along, or adding pictures or tactile symbols for non-readers.

- Switch-adapted toys: Toys that run on batteries may be adapted to be operated by the use of a switch, thus providing the student with limited physical movement the ability to play with the toy.

Seating and Positioning

Adaptive seating systems and positioning devices provide students with appropriate positioning to enhance participation and access to the curriculum. Seating and positioning systems may include seat inserts for wheelchairs, standers, and adaptive chairs, as well as inflated "pillows" or "wiggle seats" for helping children with ADHD remain seated.

Visual Aids

Visual aids include magnifiers, talking calculators, Braille writers, adapted tape players, screen reading software applications, and Braille note-taking devices that assist a student with a visual impairment to access and produce information in a print format.

- **Braille writer:** A portable device for producing Braille. Students type in text on the keyboard, using the six key entry method. A copy of the text in Braille is embossed on the paper inserted into the Braille writer.

- **Electronic Braille writer:** A updated version of the Braille writer, the electronic Braille writer is lightweight and offers the option of the text being read aloud to the student. A Braille copy of the text can also be printed out.

- **Closed circuit television (CCTV):** Assists students with visual impairments by enlarging text and graphics. The page to be read is placed on the base under the camera. The image is displayed on a monitor, with an appropriate level of magnification for the student. Foreground and background colors can be altered for the individual student.

- **Text enlargement software:** Software is available to increase the size of the text and graphics displayed on the computer monitor.

- **Screen reading software:** Screen reading software may also be of benefit to students with visual impairments. These applications allow the computer to read the text aloud.

A student with a disability may require AT in a variety of categories. For example, a student may use an augmentative communication device to supplement communication skills, adaptive-switch toys to participate in leisure activities, and an adapted keyboard for accessing software applications on the classroom computer.

AT devices are not limited to specific disability areas. For example, a student with an attention deficit may require an assistive listening device to focus attention on the teacher's voice. Students with various types of disabilities may benefit from audio-recorded materials that were originally developed for students with visual impairments.

The IEP committee determines the need for AT devices and services. Most school districts have policies/procedures regarding AT assessments and have teams of professionals that conduct the evaluation. Often the assessment team will include physical or occupational therapists and speech therapists to address communication and physical needs. The student's teacher(s) and parents are often included in the AT evaluation. Once it has been determined that an AT device or service is needed, the student's IEP team should document the required device(s) in the IEP.

The use of AT may decrease the amount of other support services a student needs to be successful.

In addition to providing the devices, IDEA requires services to support the AT devices. IDEA '97 defines AT services as "any service that directly assists a child with a disability in the selection, acquisition, or use of an assistive technology device." There are a variety of services included in this category.

- Evaluation: A functional evaluation of the child's needs in his or her customary environment

- Acquisition: Whether by purchasing or leasing, the local education agency is required to acquire the device for the student at no cost to the parent.

- Selection and maintenance of the AT device: Included in this area could be the design, fitting, customizing, adapting, repairing, or replacing as needed to support the needs of the child.

- Coordination with other therapies or interventions, including existing education and rehabilitation plans and programs

- Training or technical assistance for the student, the family, school personnel, employers, or anyone who provides service to the student with a disability

Suggestions about selecting and using software were given by Male (1994). First, make sure there is a curriculum correspondence between what students are working on at their desks and what they do at the computers, or whatever AT device is in use. This should follow what he calls stages of learning. Then, make certain the students proceed through the five stages of learning. Computer software should be selected with the following stages in mind:

Acquisition	Introduction of a new skill
Proficiency	Practice under supervision to achieve accuracy and speed
Maintenance	Continued practice without further instruction
Generalization	Application of the new skills in new settings and situations
Adaptation	Modifications of the task to meet new needs and demands of varying situations

Computer-Assisted Instruction

Computers are used to provide a safe, stimulating learning environment for many youth. The computer does not evaluate or offer subjective opinions about the student's work. It merely provides feedback about the correctness or incorrectness of each answer in a series. The computer is like an effective teacher when it

- Provides immediate attention and feedback
- Individualizes to the particular skill level
- Allows students to work at their own pace
- Makes corrections quickly
- Produces a professional-looking product
- Keeps accurate records on correct and error rates
- Ignores inappropriate behavior
- Focuses on the particular response
- Is nonjudgmental (Smith & Luckasson, 1992)

Computers are useful in helping teach traditional academic subjects such as math, reading, spelling, geography, and science. Effective teachers allow for drill and practice on the computer, monitor student progress, and reinforce appropriately. When students have mastered a particular level, these teachers help them progress to another level. Reasoning and problem solving are other skill areas that teachers have discovered can be taught using computers.

One type of newly developed computer software is the program Hypertext. It enables further explanation of textbook material. The explanation is accessed by a simple press of a key while the student is working on the learning material. For example, by pressing a single key, students can access definitions of difficult vocabulary words, reworded complicated text, additional detailed maps, and further information about concepts being introduced in the text. By using this program, teachers can help students by creating individualized lessons. Students with learning disabilities especially benefit.

Computer games can enhance learning skills and provide a highly desired reinforcement opportunity. When played alone, the games serve as leisure activities for the individual. When played with classmates, the games can help develop interpersonal relationships. Use of computer games is particularly applicable to youngsters with behavioral disorders and learning and intellectual disabilities, as well as those without any identified disability.

Word Processing Technology and the Process Approach

The process approach to writing is encouraged, especially when using a word processor (Male, 1994). These stages include planning and prewriting, drafting, revising and editing, and sharing and publication. Progressing through these stages is particularly helpful for developing writers.

The planning stage is characterized by written outlines, brainstorming, clustering or mind mapping, and lists of ideas, themes, or key words. These activities are ideally suited to a classroom that has a large television monitor or a computer projection device so that the teacher can list, group, revise, and expand ideas as students share them. Printed copies of what was generated by the group can be distributed at the end of the class session.

In the drafting stage, individuals can do draft work at a computer by themselves, or they can collaborate as a group on the work. Some students may choose to use pencil and paper to do initial draft work, or they may want to dictate stories to the teacher or another student who writes it down for them, or to voice-to-text computer software.

Students share their work during the revising and editing stage. Students read their stories aloud to a partner, a small group, or the whole class. Classmates are instructed to ask questions and give feedback that will help the writer make revisions to the work. After the content of the story has been completed, attention is given to mechanics and writing conventions. Specific software designed to aid each of these tasks is available.

The sharing and publication stage enables students to experience being authors responding to an audience. Students are encouraged to share their work by reading it aloud and distributing it in printed form. They can do this with or without graphics or illustrations.

SKILL 3.7 Instructional strategies/techniques that support transition goals

Essential Domains of Transition Planning for Students with Disabilities

One of the requirements of a student's IEP is that transition services be included. Transition services will be different for each student. Transition services must take into account the student's interests and preferences. Evaluation of career interests, aptitudes, skills, and training may be considered.

The transition activities that have to be addressed, unless the IEP team finds it unnecessary, are instruction, community experiences, and the development of objectives related to employment and other post-school areas.

Instruction

The instruction part of the transition plan deals with school instruction. The student should have a completed portfolio upon graduation. Students should research and plan for further education and training after high school. Education can be in a college setting, technical school, or vocational center. Goals and objectives created for this transition domain depend upon the nature and severity of the student's disability, the student's interests in further education, plans made for accommodations needed in future education and training, and identification of postsecondary institutions that offer the requested training or education.

Community experiences

This part of the transition plan investigates how the student uses community resources. Resources include places for recreation, transportation services, agencies, and advocacy services. It is essential for students to deal with the following areas:

- **Recreation and leisure:** Movies, YMCA, religious activities
- **Personal and social skills:** Calling friends, religious groups, going out to eat
- **Mobility and transportation:** Passing a driver's license test or using Dial-A-Ride
- **Agency access:** Using a phone book and making calls
- **System advocacy:** Have a list of advocacy groups to contact
- **Citizenship and legal issues:** For example, registering to vote

Development of employment

This segment of the transition plan investigates becoming employed. Students should complete a career interest inventory. They should have chances to investigate different careers. Many work-skill activities can take place within the classroom, home, and community. Classroom activities may concentrate on employability skills, community skills, mobility, and vocational training. Home and neighborhood activities may concentrate on personal responsibility and daily chores. Community-based activities may focus on part-time work after school and in the summer, cooperative education or work-study, individualized vocational training, and volunteer work.

Daily living skills

This segment of the transition plan is also important, although it may not be included in all IEPs, depending upon the needs of the student. For some students with disabilities, however, living away from home can be an enormous undertaking. Numerous skills are needed to live and function as an adult. In order to live as independently as possible, a person should have an income; know how to cook, clean, shop, pay bills, and get to a job; and have a social life. Some living situations may entail independent living, shared living with a roommate, supported living, or group homes. Areas that may need to be looked into include personal and social skills, living options, income and finances, medical needs, community resources, and transportation.

Resources to help students function effectively in a variety of environments

Vocational training is an important element in transition programs. One of the first steps in determining the appropriate vocational program entails performing a functional vocational evaluation. This evaluation gives information about a student's aptitudes, interests, and skills in relation to employment. It concentrates on practical skills related to a specific job or goal that a student has. It entails information that is collected through situational assessments while the student is on the job. These assessments may include surveys, observations, interviews, and other methods. The information obtained during the evaluation is used to define the transition activities needed for the students.

One of the first steps in determining the appropriate vocational program entails performing a functional vocational evaluation.

It also provides information on the student's strengths and weaknesses in the vocational area. It includes suggestions regarding potential career paths and training programs that are deemed appropriate for the student, makes the preparation for vocational education more precise, and minimizes the possibility that the student might enter an vocational program that doesn't reflect the student's likes or strengths.

Vocational educators that have knowledge of vocational training and job requirements can help provide career information to students. They can also help develop realistic assessment activities for students to determine if they have the aptitude or skills necessary to complete a particular program.

The transitional plan in the IEP should reflect appropriate vocational training that appeals to the student's aptitude, skills, strengths, and preferences. It should be based on decisions involving a variety of people, including the student, the family, teachers, vocational educators, and other interested parties.

Career Development

Career development is the complex process of acquiring the knowledge, skills, and attitudes necessary to create a plan of choosing and being successful in a particular career field. Career development typically has four stages. The stages of career development are awareness, exploration, preparation, and placement.

Career Awareness

Career awareness activities focus on introducing students to the broad range of career options. First, students must be provided with current, in-depth information about careers. This information includes job-related skills, necessary education and training, and a description of typical duties, responsibilities, and tasks. Students must be instructed on how to access the variety of available resources, such as Internet, professional magazines, newspapers, and periodicals. Guest speakers and career fairs are provided so that students can speak with and interview workers with first-hand experiences.

Career Exploration

Career exploration focuses on learning about careers through direct, hands-on activities. This stage is also important for gaining insight into the characteristics of these occupations as well as personal interests and strengths. These activities can be provided through in-school and work-based experiences. In-school activities include contextual learning activities, simulated work experiences, and career fairs. Work-based experiences range from non-paid to paid activities. These activities include job shadowing, mentors, company tours, internships, service learning, cooperative education, and independent study.

Career Preparation

Career preparation provides students with the specific academic and technical knowledge and skills needed for success in a particular occupation. This preparation may include career and technical education programs or postsecondary education. They include the core activities of career assessments (formal and informal) and work-readiness skills (soft-skills development, computer competency, and job search skills). Community organizations, employers, and professional organizations are also available to provide trainings and insight on accommodations that may be provided for students with special needs.

Career Placement

Students transitioning from high school need to work collaboratively with involved parents, teachers, and guidance counselors to enter either the workplace or postsecondary education successfully. Placement should depend on the student's aptitude, skills, experiences, and interests.

SKILL 3.8 Preventive strategies and intervention strategies for at-risk learners

Instructional modifications should be tried in an attempt to accommodate the student in the regular classroom. Effective instruction is geared toward individual needs and recognizes differences in how students learn. Modifications are tailored to individual student needs. Some strategies for modifying regular classroom instruction shown in the following table are effective with at-risk students with disabilities or behavior problems.

STRATEGIES FOR MODIFYING CLASSROOM INSTRUCTION	
Strategy 1	Provide active learning experiences to teach concepts. Student motivation is increased when students can manipulate, weigh, measure, read, or write using materials and skills that relate to their daily lives.
Strategy 2	Provide ample opportunities for guided practice of new skills. Frequent feedback on performance is essential to overcome student feelings of inadequacy. Peer tutoring and cooperative projects provide non-threatening practice opportunities. Individual student conferences, curriculum-based tests, and small group discussions are three useful methods for checking progress.
Strategy 3	Provide multisensory learning experiences. Students with learning problems sometimes have sensory processing difficulties; for instance, an auditory discrimination problem may cause misunderstanding about teacher expectations. Lessons and directions that include visual, auditory, tactile, and kinesthetic modes are preferable to a single-sensory approach.
Strategy 4	Present information in a manner that is relevant to the student. Particular attention to this strategy is needed when there is a cultural or economic gap between the lives of teachers and students. Relate instruction to a youngster's daily experience and interests.
Strategy 5	Provide students with concrete illustrations of their progress. Students with learning problems need frequent reinforcement for their efforts. Charts, graphs, and check sheets provide tangible markers of student achievement.

DOMAIN IV
ASSESSMENT

PERSONALIZED STUDY PLAN

KNOWN MATERIAL/ SKIP IT

PAGE	SKILL		
89	4.1	Effective and appropriate evidence-based assessments	☐
	4.2	Define and use various assessments	☐
	4.3	Interpret assessment results	☐
	4.4	Understand and use the results of assessments	☐

SKILL 4.1 Effective and appropriate evidence-based assessments

Several authors have identified principles useful in selecting, designing, and interpreting assessments in the classroom.

Linn and Gronlund (1995) identify five principles of assessment:

1. Clearly specifying what is to be assessed has priority in the assessment process

2. An assessment procedure should be selected because of its relevance to the characteristics or performance to be measured

3. Comprehensive assessment requires a variety of procedures

4. Proper use of assessment procedures requires an awareness of their limitations

5. Assessment is a means to an end, not an end in itself

Stiggins (1997) introduces seven guiding principles for classroom assessment:

1. Assessments require clear thinking and effective communication

2. Classroom assessment is key

3. Students are assessment users

4. Clear and appropriate targets are essential

5. High-quality assessment is a must

6. Understanding personal implication is essential

7. Assessment is a teaching and learning tool

Drummond lists six critical questions to ask about possible assessments when making a choice among them:

1. What specific assessment judgments and decisions have to be made?

2. What information is needed to make the best decisions?

3. What information is already available?

4. What assessment methods and instruments will provide the needed information?

5. How should appropriate instruments be located?

6. What criteria should be used in selecting and evaluating assessment instruments?

Measures of Metacognitive Function

METACOGNITION: the advanced cognitive ability to think about thinking and learning—the degree to which a student is aware of his or her own learning strategies and processes

METACOGNITION is the advanced cognitive ability to think about thinking and learning—the degree to which a student is aware of his or her own learning strategies and processes. Teachers can use informal process measures to gain information about a student's metacognitive knowledge associated with a particular task, such as analyzing visual aids. The teacher can give the student a task involving analysis of visual aids, then interview the student with direct and open-ended questions. In these interviews, the teacher attempts to answer the following three questions:

1. What does the student know about the metacognitive processes involved in using visual aids? This addresses the student's knowledge of the function of visual aids and whether the student uses background knowledge to predict or clarify the information in the visual aid.

2. If the student knows that certain strategies are needed to analyze an aid, does the student know how to employ those strategies?

3. What variables influence the student's ability or lack of ability to make efficient use of process strategies?

A teacher-made process assessment can be done with a visual aid and a structured, teacher-prepared interview. Interviews begin with global or general questions that measure what the student knows without being prompted to recall specific techniques. Examples of global or general questions are:

- What types of information can graphics tell you?

- What sorts of things make graphics useful?

- What should you do if you cannot figure out a graphic?

Following the global/general questions, the teacher can move on to specific questions about specific strategies and components of the strategies, Examples of specific questions would be:

- What does *identify what is important* mean?

- What does *activating knowledge* mean?

Beginning with general questions lessens the possibility that the student will answer what he believes the teacher wants to hear. During the specific question stage, the teacher can explore specific aspects of the student's use of the process in more detail.

Other Useful Informal Assessments

Anecdotal records

These records are notes recorded by the teacher concerning an area of interest or concern with a particular student. They should focus on observable behaviors and should be descriptive in nature. They should not include assumptions or speculations regarding affective areas such as motivation or interest. These records are usually compiled over a period of several days to several weeks.

Portfolio assessment

The use of student portfolios for some aspects of assessment has become quite common. The purpose, nature, and policies of portfolio assessment vary greatly from one setting to another. In general, though, a student's portfolio contains samples of work collected over an extended period. The nature of the subject, age of the student, and scope of the portfolio all contribute to the specific mechanics of analyzing, synthesizing, and otherwise evaluating the portfolio contents.

In most cases, the student and teacher make joint decisions as to which work samples go into the student's portfolio. A collection of work compiled over an extended time allows teacher, student, and parents to view the student's progress from a unique perspective. Qualitative changes over time can be readily apparent from work samples. Such changes are difficult to establish with strictly quantitative records typical of the scores recorded in the teacher's grade book.

Questioning

One of the most frequently occurring forms of assessment in the classroom is oral questioning by the teacher. As the teacher questions the students, she collects a great deal of information about the degree of student learning and potential sources of confusion for the students. While questioning is often viewed as a component of instructional methodology, it is also a powerful assessment tool.

SKILL 4.2 Define and use various assessments

ASSESSMENT is the gathering of information in order to make decisions. In education, assessments typically focus on student performance, progress, and behavior.

> **ASSESSMENT:** the gathering of information in order to make decisions; in education, assessments typically focus on student performance, progress, and behavior

Purposes of Assessment

In the education of students with exceptionalities, assessment is used to make decisions about the following:

- Screening and initial identification of children who may need services

- Diagnosis of specific learning disabilities

- Selection and evaluation of teaching strategies and programs

- Determination of the child's present level of performance in academics

- Classification and program placement

- Development of goals, objectives, and evaluation for the IEP

- Eligibility for a program

- Continuation of a program

- Effectiveness of instructional programs and strategies

- Effectiveness of behavioral interventions

- Accommodations needed for mandated or classroom testing

Types of Assessment

Assessment types can be categorized in a number of ways, most commonly in terms of what is being assessed, how the assessment is constructed, or how it is to be used. It is important to understand these differences so as to be able to correctly interpret assessment results.

Formal vs. informal

This variable focuses on how the assessment is constructed or scored. **FORMAL ASSESSMENTS** are assessments such as standardized tests or textbook quizzes—objective tests that include primarily questions for which there is only one correct, easily identifiable answer. These can be commercial or teacher-made assessments, given to either groups or individuals. **INFORMAL ASSESSMENTS** have fewer objective measures and may include anecdotes or observations that may or may not be quantified, interviews, informal questioning during a task, etc. An example might be watching a student sort objects to see what attribute is most important to the student, or questioning a student to see what he or she found confusing about a task.

Standardized tests

Standardized tests are formal tests that are administered to either groups or individuals in a specifically prescribed manner, with strict rules to keep procedures, scoring,

FORMAL ASSESSMENTS: assessments such as standardized tests or textbook quizzes—objective tests that include primarily questions for which there is only one correct, easily identifiable answer

INFORMAL ASSESSMENTS: assessments that have fewer objective measures, and may include anecdotes or observations that may or may not be quantified, interviews, informal questioning during a task, etc.

and interpretation of results uniform in all cases. Such tests allow comparisons to be made across populations, across ages or grades, or over time for a particular student. Intelligence tests and most diagnostic tests are standardized tests.

Norm-referenced vs. criterion-referenced

This distinction is based on the standard to which the student's performance is being compared. Norm-referenced tests establish a ranking and compare the student's performance to an established norm, usually for age or grade peers. What the student knows is of less importance than how similar the student's performance is to a specific group. Norm-referenced tests are, by definition, standardized. Examples include intelligence tests and many achievement tests. Norm-referenced tests are often used in determining eligibility for special needs services. Criterion-referenced tests measure a student's knowledge of specific content, usually related to classroom instruction. The student's performance is compared to a set of criteria or a preestablished standard of information the student is expected to know. On these tests, what the student knows is more important than how he or she compares to other students. Examples include math quizzes at the end of a chapter, or some state-mandated tests of specific content. Criterion-referenced tests are used to determine whether a student has mastered required skills.

Group vs. individual assessments

This variable simply refers to the manner of presentation, whether given to a group of students or on a one to one basis. Group assessments can be formal or informal, standardized or not, criterion- or norm-referenced. Individual assessments can be found in all these types as well.

Authentic assessments

Authentic assessments are designed to be as close to real life as possible so they are relevant and meaningful to the student's life. They can be formal or informal, depending upon how they are constructed. An example of an authentic test item would be calculating a 20 percent sales discount on a popular clothing item after the student has studied math percentages.

Rating scales and checklists

Rating scales and checklists are generally self-appraisal instruments completed by the student or observation-based instruments completed by teacher or parents. The focus is frequently on behavior or affective areas such as interest, motivation, attention or depression. These tests can be formal or informal and some can be standardized and norm-referenced. Examples of norm-referenced tests of this type would be ADHD rating scales or the Behavior Assessment System for Children.

Screening, diagnosis, and placement

Intelligence tests have historically been considered relatively good predictors of school performance. These tests are standardized and norm referenced. Examples are the Wechsler Intelligence Scale for Children—Fourth Edition (WISC-IV), Stanford-Binet IV, and Kaufman Assessment Battery for Children—Second Edition (KACB-II). Some intelligence tests are designed for use with groups and are used for screening and identification purposes. The individual tests are used for classification and program placement. Since intelligence is a quality that is difficult to define precisely, results of intelligence tests should not be used to discriminate or define the person's potential. In recent years, intelligence testing has evolved to include measures of multiple intelligences (Gardner, 1999) and these tests can further refine placement decisions for students with special needs. In many cases a significant discrepancy between scores on different intelligences helps to identify specific learning disabilities. Such measures also help show how a disability impacts performance in different areas of the curriculum.

There are many standardized achievement and educational skills tests, including state-mandated testing, that are also used by school systems to help determine eligibility and placement.

Standardized tests will have very specific instructions regarding procedures for administration, and it is the teacher's responsibility to see that these standardized procedures are followed. Failure to follow them will invalidate the resulting scores and make it impossible to correctly interpret the results. Some standardized tests also have lists of accommodations that can be used for students with special needs, and these must be carefully recorded and rules about their use strictly followed.

Even with informal assessments, teachers should be attentive to the procedures for administration and at least record differences in administration to different students so results can be correctly interpreted.

It is important for the teacher to correctly interpret the results of any formal assessments used. Most standardized tests will explain how to interpret results so the teacher does not make errors and assume that a test result means something it does not mean.

Particular care must be taken in interpreting some tests. Intelligence test scores, for example, should be interpreted in terms of performance and not the person's potential. The teacher must read the test manuals and become familiar with the following items:

- Areas measured: Verbal, quantitative, memory, cognitive skills, or the multiple intelligences on some assessments

- Population: Target age groups, lack of cultural bias, adaptations or norms for children with physical handicaps such as blindness

- Standardization information: Mean and standard deviation, scaled scores and what they mean

- Means of comparing performance among subtests, such as the Verbal and Performance IQ scores of the WISC-IV

- Uses of the results: The test manual will contain information about how the results can be used (e.g., using the K-ABC-II to identify gifted children), or how they are not to be used (e.g., assuming that a third grade student who gets a score like a fifth grader on a third grade test is ready to do fifth grade work—an assumption that would not be correct)

- Information on use with special populations, such as Spanish-speaking students, or students with visual impairments, physical impairments, or learning disabilities

- Information concerning reliability and validity

Behavioral and Emotional Assessment

Standardized measures of behavior involve direct observation with a behavior rating scale. Measurement of emotional state involves inference and subjectivity on the part of the examiner.

Behavior rating scales

Examples of these scales are the Revised Behavior Problem Checklist, Behavior Rating Profile, and Burks Behavior Rating Scales. Items may be grouped according to categorical characteristics. For the Revised Behavior Problem Checklist, the four major scales are Conduct Disorder, Socialized Aggression, Attention Problem-Immaturity, and Anxiety-Withdrawn, with minor scales of Psychotic Behavior and Motor Excess. Behavior-rating scales require that the examiner rate examples of behaviors on Likert-type scales, such as 0 = not a problem, 1 = mild problem, and 2 = severe problem.

Each scale has its own set of scoring procedures. Therefore, the teacher must be sure to consult the test manual before attempting to interpret the results. The following are other factors to consider in interpreting behavior-rating scales:

- Reliability and validity information: Norm group information and relevant research on the test instrument

- Sources of information: Some tests include parent and youth reports or measure behavior across a number of settings in and out of school

- Suggested uses of the results: Some tests are intended for screening but not diagnostic purposes
- Scoring and profile information: For example, the Child Behavior Checklist and Revised Behavior Profile lists three social competency scales and behavior problem scales identified by factor analysis for boys and girls in three separate age ranges

Measures of emotional state

These tests are designed to be administered by trained psychologists and psychiatrists. The child's emotional state is inferred by analyzing observable behavior. Types of tests include projective methods, measures of self-concept, and inventories and questionnaires.

Projective methods

The theory behind these methods is that a person will project his or her own meaning, patterns, feelings, and significance onto ambiguous stimuli. Because these tests are subjective, it is difficult to establish reliability and validity; therefore, their usefulness for educational purposes is limited. Some examples of these tests are:

- Rorschach ink blot test: The individual states what he "sees" in each of the ten inkblots. Diagnostic interpretation is based on clinical data.
- Thematic apperception test: The examiner uses a series of thirty-one pictures and asks the child to tell a story about them. The examiner looks for themes in the stories, especially those relating to the main character.

When interpreting these tests, attention must be paid to the reliability and validity, the training of the examiner, and the subjective quality.

Self-concept measures

Some familiar examples are the Tennessee Self-Concept Scale and Piers-Harris Children's Self-Concept Scale. Most instruments use a system of self-evaluation and self-report. Therefore, the child might choose the answer that he or she believes the examiner wants to see. In addition, because self-concept is a difficult construct to define, there is the problem of adequate validity.

Inventories and questionnaires

Many of these are designed for measuring the emotional and personality characteristics of adolescents and adults. These tests are often self-reported, although some, such as the Personality Inventory for Children (PIC), include a parent report. Results are grouped into such scales as adjustment, achievement, depression, delinquency, and anxiety. These results are generally used with classification and placement decisions. Reliability and validity should be considered when interpreting these tests.

The PIC was designed specifically for evaluating children. The parent completes the true/false items, and three validity scales are included to determine the truthfulness of the responses. Thirteen of the thirty scales are considered the profile scales, with the first three—adjustment, achievement, and intellectual screening—considered the cognitive triad.

SKILL 4.3   Interpret assessment results

The knowledge of how to interpret and apply formal and informal assessment data is very important to the development of IEPs. An IEP is designed around the child's strengths and weaknesses, so it is critical to correctly interpret the implications of assessment data to determine those strengths and weaknesses.

Results of formal, standardized assessments are given in derived scores, which compare the student's raw score to the performance of a specified group of subjects. Criteria for the selection of the group may be based on characteristics of age, sex, or geographic area. The test results of formal assessments must always be interpreted in light of what type of tasks the individual was required to perform and the "norm" group to which he/she is being compared. The most commonly used derived scores are as follows:

AGE AND GRADE EQUIVALENTS are considered developmental scores because they attempt to convert the student's raw score into an average performance of a particular age or grade group.

QUARTILES, DECILES, AND PERCENTILES indicate the percentage of scores that fall below the individual's raw score. Quartiles divide the score into four equal parts; the first quartile is the point at which 25 percent of the scores fall below the full score. Deciles divide the distribution into ten equal parts; the seventh decile would mark the point below which 70 percent of the scores fall. Percentiles are the most frequently used. A percentile rank of 45 would indicate that the person's raw score was at the point below which 45 percent of the other scores fell.

STANDARD SCORES are raw scores with the same mean (average) and standard deviation (variability of asset of scores). In the standardization of a test, about 68 percent of the scores will fall above or below one standard deviation of the mean of 100. About 96 percent of the scores will fall within the range of two standard

AGE AND GRADE EQUIVALENT: scores that attempt to convert the student's raw score into an average performance of a particular age or grade group

QUARTILES, DECILES, AND PERCENTILES: the percentage of scores that fall below the individual's raw score

STANDARD SCORES: raw scores with the same mean (average) and standard deviation (variability of asset of scores)

deviations above or below the mean. A standard deviation of 20, for example, means that 68 percent of the scores fall between 80 and 120, with 100 as the mean.

Standard scores are useful because they allow for the direct comparison of raw scores from different individuals. In interpreting scores, it is important to note what type of standard score is being used. Most standardized test manuals will explain how to interpret results so the team does not make errors and assume that a test result means something it does not mean. For example, it is important to understand that a percentile score of 45 means something very different from a score of 45% correct on a quiz. The 45% correct would probably be a failing grade, but the 45th percentile score is well within the normal range of performance.

Not only must the scores be interpreted in terms of the norm, but comparison of performance among subtests, such as the Verbal and Performance IQ scores of the WISC-IV, must be considered. IEP goals and objectives will be written for skills that are significantly below the norm or significantly below the student's typical skill level on other subtests.

Particular care must be taken in interpreting some tests. Intelligence test scores, for example, should be interpreted in terms of performance and not the person's potential. In terms of IEP development, the most useful results of any type of testing are those that pinpoint specific strengths and weaknesses, and specific learning styles and needs of the student. Global "IQ" scores or overall achievement scores are less useful than the measure of specific skills such as visual integration, working memory, or decoding skills.

RUBRIC: a list of a very specific set of behaviors or responses required for a particular level of performance

RUBRICS can be very useful in assessing components of critical skills and pinpointing areas to be included in IEP goals and objectives. A rubric simply lists a very specific set of behaviors or responses required for a particular level of performance. Using a rubric as a checklist can provide detailed information on elements of a skill that need special attention.

INVENTORY: a list of very specific skills necessary for an individual to live successfully in a particular environment

ENVIRONMENTAL OR ECOLOGICAL INVENTORIES are designed to collect information about a specific individual's natural environment so instruction can be planned that will allow that individual to be as independent as possible in that chosen environment. Such an inventory is a list of very specific skills necessary for an individual to live successfully in a particular environment. It might be the skills necessary for getting from class to class on time in high school; the skills necessary to do or even *get to* a specific job; the skills necessary to cook or do laundry, etc. The inventory is highly individualized and is based on task analyses that will enable educators to design both IEP goals and objectives and the instruction necessary to help the student meet those goals. They are important in planning adaptive behavior curricula throughout a child's educational life, but are particularly relevant as transition to adult life is being planned.

Making Instructional Decisions Based on Assessment Results

Assessment is key to providing differentiated and appropriate instruction to all students, and this is the area in which teachers will most often use assessment. Teachers should use a variety of assessment techniques to determine the existing knowledge, skills, and needs of each student. Depending on the age of the student and the subject matter under consideration, diagnosis of readiness may be accomplished through pretest, checklists, teacher observation, or student self-report. Diagnosis serves two related purposes—to identify those students who are not ready for the new instruction and to identify for each student what prerequisite knowledge is lacking.

Student assessment is an integral part of the teaching-learning process. Identifying student, teacher, or program weaknesses is only significant if the information so obtained is used to remedy those concerns. Lesson materials and lesson delivery must be evaluated to determine relevant prerequisite skills and abilities. The teacher must be capable of determining whether a student's difficulties lie with the new information, with a lack of significant prior knowledge, or with a core learning disability that must be addressed with specialized lesson plans or accommodations. The ultimate goal of any diagnostic or assessment endeavor is improved learning. Thus, instruction is adapted to the needs of the learner based on assessment information.

Using Assessment Information to Modify Plans and Adapt Instruction

Assessment skills should be an integral part of teacher training. Teachers are able to use pre- and post-assessments of content areas to monitor student learning, analyze assessment data in terms of individualized support for students and instructional practice for teachers, and design lesson plans that have measurable outcomes and definitive learning standards. Assessment information should be used to provide performance-based criteria and academic expectations for all students in evaluating whether students have learned the expected skills and content of the subject area.

> *Assessment information should be used to provide performance-based criteria and academic expectations for all students in evaluating whether students have learned the expected skills and content of the subject area.*

For example, in an Algebra I class, teachers can use assessment to see whether students have the prior knowledge to engage in the proposed lesson. If the teacher provides students with a pre-assessment on algebraic expression and ascertains whether the lesson plan should be modified to include a prealgebraic expression lesson unit to refresh student understanding of the content area, then the teacher can create, if needed, quantifiable data to support the need of additional resources to support student learning. Once the teacher has taught the unit on algebraic expression, a post-assessment test can be used to test student learning, and a mastery examination can be used to test how well students understand and can apply the knowledge to the next unit of math content learning.

A teacher working with students with learning disabilities will use assessment information in additional ways. For example, if assessments show a student has extreme difficulty organizing information in the visual field, a teacher may modify a worksheet in math to present only one problem positioned in a large, squared-off field, with lots of white space around it, or even set up problems to be presented one problem at a time on 4×6 inch cards, etc.

By making inferences on teaching methods and gathering clues for student performance, teachers can use assessment data to inform and have an impact on instructional practices.

By making inferences on teaching methods and gathering clues for student performance, teachers can use assessment data to inform and have an impact on instructional practices. By analyzing the various types of assessments, teachers can gather more definitive information on projected student academic performance. Instructional strategies for teachers would provide learning targets for student behavior, cognitive thinking skills, and processing skills that can be employed to diversify student learning opportunities.

DOMAIN V
FOUNDATIONS AND PROFESSIONAL RESPONSIBILITIES

PERSONALIZED STUDY PLAN

KNOWN MATERIAL/ SKIP IT

PAGE	SKILL		
103	5.1:	Federal definitions	☐
	5.2:	Federal requirements for the pre-referral, referral, and identification	☐
	5.3:	Federal safeguards of the rights of stakeholders	☐
	5.4:	Components of a legally defensible individualized education program	☐
	5.5:	Major legislation	☐
	5.6:	Roles and responsibilities of the special education teacher	☐
	5.7:	Roles and responsibilities of other professionals who deliver special education services	☐
	5.8:	Strengths and limitations of various collaborative approaches	☐
	5.9:	Communication with stakeholders	☐
	5.10:	Potential bias issues that may impact teaching and interactions with students and their families	☐

Background

The revision of the original law now known as IDEA included changes that were primarily in language (terminology), procedures (especially transition), and the addition of new categories (autism and traumatic brain injury). We can see that despite challenges to federal services and mandates in special education as an extension of the 14th Amendment since 1980, there has actually been growth in mandated categories and net funding. The Doctrine of Selective Incorporation is the name for one major set of challenges to this process.

While the 1994 conservative turnover in the Congress might seem to undercut the force of PL 94-132, two decades of recent history show strong bipartisan support for special education; consequently, IDEA, or a joint federal-state replacement, will most likely remain strong. Lobbyists and activists representing coalition and advocacy groups for those with disabilities combined with bipartisan congressional support to avert the proposed changes, which would have meant drastic setbacks in services for persons with disabilities.

Nevertheless, there remain several philosophical controversies in special education. The need for labels for categories continues to be questioned. Many states are serving special needs students by severity level rather than by the exceptionality category.

Special needs educators are faced with possible changes in what is considered to be the least restrictive environment for educating students with special needs. Following upon the heels of the Regular Education Initiative, the concept of inclusion has come to the forefront. Both of these movements were, and are, an attempt to educate special needs students in the mainstream of the regular classroom. Both would eliminate pulling students out of regular classroom instructional activities, and both would incorporate the services of special education teachers in the regular classroom in collaboration with general classroom teachers.

Special education has changed significantly in recent decades. From separated, specialized classrooms for virtually every area of disability, special education has moved into the world of inclusion and undergone stricter accountability for general education learning standards.

According to IDEA 2004, special education students are to participate in general education programs to the fullest extent from which they can receive benefit. This often means accommodations and modifications in class work, employment of classroom assistants, and, in some cases, individual care aides. It also means there

IDEA included changes that were primarily in language (terminology), procedures (especially transition), and the addition of new categories (autism and traumatic brain injury).

According to IDEA 2004, special education students are to participate in general education programs to the fullest extent from which they can receive benefit.

needs to be a closer working relationship between the special needs educator and general education teacher. Special education services are likely to be in the form of push-in services in the general education classroom, including team teaching, or through consultation with the special educator. Fewer students are served in special education classrooms for the entire day, and resource services are used only as deemed absolutely necessary by the IEP team.

> Special educators are accountable for meeting the same learning standards as general educators.

Special educators are accountable for meeting the same learning standards as general educators. No Child Left Behind (NCLB) stipulates that students are expected to read by grade three, requiring the use of a variety of reading methods (including phonics) to that end. In addition, all students are expected to show adequate yearly progress (AYP) as measured by the same standardized tests used in general education. In very few cases, when the disability is severe, the student may be given alternate assessment.

Definitions

IDEA 2004 §300.8 defines a child with a disability as "having mental retardation, a hearing impairment (including deafness), a speech or language impairment, a visual impairment (including blindness), a serious emotional disturbance (referred to in this part as emotional disturbance), an orthopedic impairment, autism, traumatic brain injury, another health impairment, a specific learning disability, deaf-blindness, or multiple disabilities, and who, by reason thereof, needs special education and related services."

Eligibility for special education services is based on a student having one of the above disabilities (or a combination thereof) and a demonstration of educational need through professional evaluation. Simply having one of these conditions does not in itself qualify a child as having a disability under this law. The condition must prevent a child from being able to benefit from regular education.

The classification of exceptional student education is a categorical system. Within the categories are subdivisions which may be based on the severity or level of support services needed. Having a categorical system allows educators to differentiate and define types of disabilities, relate treatments to certain categories, and concentrate research and advocacy efforts. The disadvantage of the categorical system is the labeling of groups or individuals. Critics of labels say that labeling can place the emphasis on the label and not the individual needs of the child. The following table displays the current definitions of disabilities.

DEFINITIONS OF DISABILITIES UNDER IDEA 2004	
Autism	A developmental disability significantly affecting verbal and nonverbal communication and social interaction, generally evident before age three, that adversely affects a child's educational performance. Other characteristics often associated with autism are engagement in repetitive activities and stereotyped movements, resistance to environmental change or change in daily routines, and unusual responses to sensory experiences. Autism does not apply if a child's educational performance is adversely affected primarily because the child has an emotional disturbance A child who manifests the characteristics of autism after age three could be identified as having autism if the above two indicators are present.
Deaf	A hearing impairment that is so severe that the child is impaired in processing linguistic information through hearing, with or without amplification, that adversely affects a child's educational performance.
Deaf-blind	The concomitant hearing and visual impairments, the combination of which causes such severe communication and other developmental and educational needs that they cannot be accommodated in special education programs solely for children with deafness or children with blindness.
Emotional Disturbance	Schizophrenia, and conditions in which 1 or more of these characteristics is exhibited over a long period of time and to a marked degree: (a) inability to learn not explained by intellectual, sensory, or health factors, (b) inability to build or maintain satisfactory interpersonal relationships, (c) inappropriate types of behavior or feelings, (d) general pervasive unhappiness or depression, (e) tendency to develop physical symptoms or fears associated with personal or school problems.
Hearing Impairment	An impairment in hearing, whether permanent or fluctuating, that adversely affects a child's educational performance but that is not included under the definition of deafness in this section.
Mentally Retarded	A significantly subaverage general intellectual functioning, existing concurrently with deficits in adaptive behavior and manifested during the developmental period, that adversely affects a child's educational performance.
Multiple Disabilities	Concomitant impairments (such as mental retardation-blindness, mental retardation-orthopedic impairment, etc.), the combination of which causes such severe educational needs that they cannot be accommodated in special education programs solely for one of the impairments. The term does not include deaf-blindness.

Continued on next page

Orthopedic Impairment	A severe orthopedic impairment that adversely affects a child's educational performance. The term includes impairments caused by a congenital anomaly (e.g., clubfoot, absence of some member, etc.), impairments caused by disease (e.g., poliomyelitis, bone tuberculosis, etc.), and impairments from other causes (e.g., cerebral palsy, amputations, and fractures or burns that cause contractures).
Other Health Impairment	Having limited strength, vitality, or alertness, including a heightened alertness to environmental stimuli, that results in limited alertness with respect to the educational environment, that: is due to chronic or acute health problems such as asthma, attention deficit disorder or attention deficit hyperactivity disorder, diabetes, epilepsy, a heart condition, hemophilia, lead poisoning, leukemia, nephritis, rheumatic fever, sickle cell anemia, or Tourette's syndrome; and adversely affects a child's educational performance.
Specific Learning Disability	This term means a disorder in one or more of the basic psychological processes involved in understanding or in using language, spoken or written, that may manifest itself in an imperfect ability to listen, think, speak, read, write, spell, or do mathematical calculations, including conditions such as perceptual disabilities, brain injury, minimal brain dysfunction, dyslexia, and developmental aphasia. **Disorders not included:** The term does not include learning problems that are primarily the result of visual, hearing, or motor disabilities, of mental retardation, of emotional disturbance, or of environmental, cultural, or economic disadvantage.
Speech or Language Impairment	A communication disorder, such as stuttering, impaired articulation, a language impairment, or a voice impairment, that adversely affects a child's educational performance.
Traumatic Brain Injury	An acquired injury to the brain caused by an external physical force resulting in total or partial functional disability or psychosocial impairment, or both, that adversely affects a child's educational performance. The term applies to open or closed head injuries resulting in impairments in one or more areas, such as cognition, language, memory, attention, reasoning, abstract thinking, judgment, problem-solving, sensory, perceptual and motor abilities, psychosocial behavior, physical functions, information processing, and speech. The term does not apply to brain injuries that are congenital or degenerative or to brain injuries induced by birth trauma.
Visual Impairment including Blindness	An impairment in vision that, even with correction, adversely affects a child's educational performance. The term includes both partial sight and blindness.

It should be noted that there is no classification for gifted children under IDEA. Funding and services for gifted programs are left up to the individual states and school districts. Therefore, the number of districts providing services and the scope of gifted programs varies among states and school districts.

Seldom does a student with a disability fall into only one of the categories listed in IDEA 2004. For example, a student with a hearing impairment may also have a specific learning disability, or a student on the autism spectrum may also demonstrate a specific language impairment. In fact, language impairment is inherent in autism. Sometimes, the eligibility is defined as multiple disabilities (with one listed as a primary eligibility on the IEP, and the others listed as secondary). Sometimes there are overlapping needs that are not necessarily listed as a secondary disability.

SKILL 5.2 Federal requirements for the pre-referral, referral, and identification

Public Law (PL) 94-142 (Education for the Handicapped Act) was signed in 1975 and renamed Individuals with Disabilities Education Act (IDEA) in 1990. This law, in its various forms and revisions, lies at the foundation of all current special education practices. It was a culmination of many years' struggle to achieve equal educational opportunity for children and youth with disabilities.

The 1960s was an era when much national emphasis was placed upon the civil rights of the U.S. citizenry. Special education was supported by such leaders as President John F. Kennedy, Vice President Hubert Humphrey, President Lyndon B. Johnson, and many more in Congress. Unlike rights legislation of a racial or an ethnic nature, the reform laws for persons with disabilities mostly enjoyed bipartisan support. From the late 1960s to the mid-1970s, much legislation and litigation from the courts included decisions supporting the need to assure an appropriate education to all persons, regardless of race, creed, or disabling conditions. Much of what was stated in separate court rulings and mandated legislation was brought together into what is now considered to be the "backbone" of special education, PL 94-142, which was formally signed into law by President Gerald R. Ford in 1975.

The philosophy behind these pieces of legislation is that education is to be provided to all children who meet age eligibility requirements. All children are assumed capable of benefiting from education. For children with severe or profound handicaps, education may be interpreted to include training in basic self-help skills, as well as vocational training and academics.

Although IDEA has been revised several times since its inception, its basic principles in all forms incorporate the concept of normalization. Within this concept, persons with disabilities have access to everyday patterns and conditions of life that are as close as possible or equal to their peers without disabilities. IDEA includes the following fundamental provisions:

1. **Free appropriate public education (FAPE):** Special Education services are to be provided at no cost to students or their families. The federal and state governments share any additional costs. FAPE also requires that education be appropriate to the individual needs of the students.

2. **Notification and procedural rights for parents:** These include a number of due process principles:

   A. Right to examine records and obtain independent evaluations

   B. Right to receive a clearly written notice that states the results of the school's evaluation of the child and whether the child meets eligibility requirements for placement or continuation of special services

   C. Parents who disagree with the school's decision may request a due process hearing and a judicial hearing if they do not receive satisfaction through due process.

3. **Identification and services to all children:** States must conduct public outreach programs to seek out and identify children who may need services. This includes identifying students in the private as well as the public school setting.

4. **Necessary related services:** Developmental, corrective, and other support services that make it possible for a student to benefit from special education services must be provided. These may include speech, recreation, or physical therapy.

5. **Individualized assessments:** Evaluations and tests must be nondiscriminatory and individualized. Specifically, they must be conducted in the preferred language of the student.

6. **Individualized Education Plans:** Each student receiving special education services must have an Individualized Education Plan (IEP) developed in a meeting that includes a qualified representative of the local education agency (LEA), special education teacher(s), general education teacher(s), a person qualified to interpret assessment information, the parents, and the student (as appropriate). Others present at the meeting may include any personnel who provide services to the student, such as speech therapists or occupational therapists. The parents and/or the school may invite others to the meeting as needed. Note: It is important to remember that an IEP is a legal document that is binding on both the school and any teacher working with the child. See Skill 9.1 for details about the components of an IEP and the manner in which they can be used.

7. **Least restrictive environment (LRE):** There is no simple definition of LRE. LRE differs with the child's needs. LRE means that the student is placed in an environment that is not dangerous or overly controlling or intrusive. The student should be given opportunities to experience what other peers of similar mental or chronological age are doing. Finally, LRE is the environment that is the most integrated and normalized for the student's strengths and weaknesses. LRE for one child may be a regular classroom with support services, while LRE for another may be a self-contained classroom in a special school. The Council for Exceptional Children lists seven levels of service relevant to LRE (Adapted from Deno, 1970):

CASCADE SYSTEM OF SPECIAL EDUCATION SERVICES	
Level 1	Regular classroom, including students with disabilities able to learn with regular class accommodations, with or without medical and counseling services
Level 2	Regular classroom with supportive services (i.e., consultation, inclusion)
Level 3	Regular class with part-time special class (i.e., itinerant services, resource room)
Level 4	Full-time special class (i.e., self-contained)
Level 5	Special stations (i.e., special schools)
Level 6	Homebound
Level 7	Residential (i.e., hospital, institution)

8. **Advisory Boards:** States are required to have advisory boards composed of individuals with disabilities, teachers and parents of students with disabilities to oversee compliance.

9. **Early Intervention:** Later forms of IDEA include provision for early intervention services and Individualized Family Service Plans (IFSP) for children 0-5 years of age.

10. **Funds:** IDEA supplies supplementary funds on a per child basis, and funds can be withheld in cases of noncompliance with the law.

IDEA has been updated several times.

Section 504, a part of Public Law 93-112, was passed and signed into law in 1973. It is important because many children not covered under IDEA may be covered under Section 504. Currently Section 504 expands the older law by extending its protection to other areas that receive federal assistance, such as education. To be entitled to protection under Section 504, the individual must meet the definition of a person with a disability, which is any person who

1. Has a physical or mental impairment that substantially limits one or more of such person's major life activities

2. Has a record of such impairment

3. Is regarded as having such impairment

Major life activities include caring for one's self, performing manual tasks, walking, seeing, hearing, speaking, breathing, working, and learning.

The individual must also be otherwise qualified. This criterion has been interpreted to mean that the person must be able to meet the requirements of a particular program in spite of his or her disability. The person must be afforded reasonable accommodations by recipients of federal financial assistance. The usual remedy when a violation of Section 504 is proven is the termination of federal funding assistance.

> Section 504 assists with the several categories of children that are not comprehensively covered for special education under IDEA. Children in these categories may meet the definition for disabled but are not eligible.

Section 504 assists with the several categories of children that are not comprehensively covered for special education under IDEA. Children in these categories may meet the definition for disabled but are not eligible. For example, a child with an emotional disorder may not meet the criteria for intensity and degree. Others have medical conditions, but these conditions are not listed as disabilities. An example is the child with AIDS whose condition is not listed specifically in Other Health Impaired.

Youth with social impairments do not qualify for special education under IDEA unless they have an emotional or behavioral disorder as well. There is controversy over whether to identify or even attempt to separate youth with social maladjustments from other youth who meet the definition of emotional/behavioral disturbance. Unlike slow learners, some of whom may qualify for compensatory services, these youngsters have no safety net of services.

Attention Deficit Disorder (ADD) is another category of children who require significant assistance in schools but for whom special education historically had no category. Recently, some states have included it under medical conditions. Youth who are addicted to drugs and alcohol are protected under IDEA only if they qualify for special education and related services under one of the disability categories such as emotional disturbance. These students, like other categories described, are at-risk, and, while they do not qualify for special education under IDEA, they are entitled to protection under Section 504 of the Rehabilitation Act or the Americans with Disabilities Act (ADA).

Section 504 requires that schools not discriminate and provide reasonable accommodations in all programming aspects.

SKILL 5.3 Federal safeguards of the rights of stakeholders

The needs of exceptional students are by definition multidisciplinary; a teacher of exceptional children often serves as the hub of a many-spoked wheel while communicating, consulting, and collaborating with the various stakeholders in a child's educational life. Managing these relationships effectively can be a challenge, but it is central to successful work in exceptional education.

Role of the Family

Understanding the role of the family will assist a new educator with involving the parents in the educational team. The presence of a child with a disability within the family unit creates changes and possible stresses that will need to be addressed. Many parents feel the demands of the disabled child are greatly in excess of a non-disabled child's requirements.

The family, as a microcosmic unit in a society, plays a vital role in many ways. The family assumes a protective and nurturing function, is the primary unit for social control, and plays a major role in the transmission of cultural values and mores. This role is enacted concurrently with changes in our social system as a whole. Paradoxically, parents who were formerly viewed as *causing* a child's disability are now depended upon to enact positive changes in their children's lives.

Parents as Advocates

Ironically, establishing the parent-educator partnership, an action that is now sought by educators around the nation, came about largely through the advocacy efforts of parents. The state compulsory education laws began in 1918. They were adopted across the nation with small variances in agricultural regions. However, due to the fact that children with disabilities did not fit in with the general school curriculum, most continued to be turned away at the schoolhouse door, leaving the custodial services at state or private institutions as the primary alternative placement site for parents.

The 1950s brought about the founding of many parent and professional organizations, and the movement continued into the next decade. Learning groups included the National Association of Parents and Friends of Mentally Retarded Children, which was founded in 1950 and later called the National Association for Retarded Children (it is now named the National Association of Retarded Citizens); the International Parents Organization, founded in 1957; and the parents' branch of the Alexander Graham Bell Association for Parents of the Deaf, founded in 1965. The Epilepsy Foundation of America was founded in 1967. The International Council for Exceptional Children had been established by faculty and students at Columbia University as early as 1922, and the Council for Exceptional Children recognized small parent organizations in the late 1940s.

During the 1950s, Public Law 85-926 brought about support for the preparation of teachers to work with children with disabilities so that these children might receive educational services.

The 1960s was the first period of time during which parents received tangible support from the executive branch of the national government. In 1960, the White House Conference on Children and Youth made the declaration that a child should be separated from his or her family only as a last resort. This gave vital support to parents' efforts toward securing a public education for their children with disabilities.

Parent groups are a major component in assuring appropriate services, to-equal with special education and community service agencies, for children with disabilities. Their role is individual and political advocacy, as well as sociopsychological support. Great advances in services for children with disabilities have been made through the efforts of parent advocacy groups. These groups have been formed to represent almost every type of disabling condition.

Parent and Professional Advocacy Activity and Parent Organization

There have always been, and will always be, exceptional children with special needs, but special education services have not always been in existence to provide for these needs. Private schools and state institutions were primary sources of education for individuals with disabilities in earlier years.

The Tenth Amendment to the U.S. Constitution leaves education as an unstated power and, therefore, vested in the states. As was the practice in Europe, government funds in America were first appropriated to experimental schools to determine whether students with disabilities actually could be educated.

During the mid-twentieth century, legislators and governors in control of funds, faced with evidence of need and the efficacy of special education programs, refused to expend funds adequately, thus creating the ultimate need for federal guidelines in PL 94-142 to mandate flow-through money. Concurrently, due process rights and procedures were outlined, based on litigation and legislation enacted by parents of children with disabilities, parent organizations, and professional advocacy groups. "Public support in the form of legislation and appropriation of funds has been achieved and sustained only by the most arduous and persevering efforts of individuals who advocate for exceptional children" (Hallahan & Kauffman, 1986 p. 26).

Parents, professionals, and other members of advocacy groups and organizations finally succeeded in bringing astounding data about the population of youth with disabilities in our country to the attention of legislators. Among the findings revealed, Congress noted that:

1. More than eight million children with disabilities were in the United States, and more than half were not receiving an appropriate education.

2. More than one million children with disabilities were excluded from the educational system, and many other children with disabilities were enrolled in regular education classes where they were not benefiting from the educational services provided because of their undetected conditions.

3. Because of inadequate educational services within the public school systems, families were forced to seek services outside the public realm. Years of advocacy effort resulted in the current laws and court decisions mandating special education at a federal level.

No Child Left Behind Legislation and Teacher Accountability

With the passing of the No Child Left Behind legislation in 2002, special education students and teachers must meet a higher standard of accountability. No Child Left Behind is designed to change the culture of America's schools by closing the achievement gap, giving more flexibility, providing parents with more options, and teaching students based on what is effective.

No Child Left Behind is designed to change the culture of America's schools by closing the achievement gap, giving more flexibility, providing parents with more options, and teaching students based on what is effective.

Under the act's accountability provisions, states must describe how they will close the achievement gap and make sure all students, including those who are disadvantaged, achieve academic proficiency. They must produce annual state and school district report cards that inform parents and communities about state and school progress. Schools that do not make progress must provide supplemental services, such as free tutoring or after-school assistance; take corrective actions; and, if still not making adequate yearly progress after five years, make dramatic changes in the way the school is run.

In an effort to ensure that states and schools are meeting educational standards, the No Child Left Behind legislation requires that each school prepare an annual district report card and give it to parents. The report cards provide information on how each school performed on state assessments. The report cards must state student performance in terms of three levels—basic, proficient, and advanced. Achievement data should be broken out by student subgroups according to race, ethnicity, gender, English language proficiency, migrant status, disability status, and low-income status. The report cards should also indicate which schools need improvement, corrective action, or restructuring.

The report cards also present information on the percentage of students not tested; graduation rates for secondary school students; performance of school districts on adequate yearly progress measures; professional qualifications of teachers in the state, including the percentage of teachers in the classroom with only emergency or provisional credentials; and the percentage of classes in the state that are not taught by highly qualified teachers, including a comparison between high- and low-income schools.

IDEA 2004 added new language that ensures that children with disabilities are taught by highly qualified teachers and receive research-based instruction. IDEA 2004 also includes new requirements that schools provide high-quality, intensive preservice preparation and professional development for all staff that work with children with disabilities.

SKILL 5.4 Components of a legally defensible individualized education program

In 1990, Congress passed Public Law 101-336, the Americans with Disabilities Act, referred to as ADA. Like the Rehabilitation Act that preceded it, ADA (1990) bars discrimination in employment, transportation, public accommodations, and telecommunications in all aspects of life. However, ADA's protection is not limited to those receiving federal funding. This act gives protection to all people without regard to race, gender, national origin, religion, or disability. Children with disabilities, therefore, automatically qualify for protection under this act.

Title ll and Title lll are applicable to special education because they cover the private sector (such as private schools) and require access to public accommodations. New and remodeled public buildings, transportation vehicles, and telephone systems now must be accessible to the persons with disabilities. ADA also protects individuals with contagious diseases, such as AIDS, from discrimination.

The ADA is similar to the Rehabilitation Act in terms of who is protected under the act, but it does not require entities to be recipients of federal financial assistance.

Public Law 105-17 (IDEA '97)

In 1997, IDEA was revised and reauthorized as Public Law 105-17 as progressive legislation for the benefit of school age children with special needs, their parents, and those who work with these children. The 1997 reauthorization of IDEA made major changes in the areas of the evaluation procedures, parent rights, transition, and discipline.

The evaluation process was amended to require that members of the evaluation team look at previously collected data, tests, and information and use it when it is deemed appropriate. Previous to IDEA '97, an entire reevaluation had to be conducted every three years to determine if the child continued to be a child with a disability. This requirement was changed so that existing information and evaluations that would prevent unnecessary assessment of students and reduce the cost of evaluations could be considered.

In addition, eligibility was redefined to require evidence not only that the child has a disability, but also that the disability has a negative impact on the child's educational success or access to equal education.

Under the previous IDEA, an evaluation team did not need parent participation to make decisions regarding a student's eligibility for special education and related services. Under IDEA '97, parents were specifically included as members of the group making the eligibility decision.

Amendments to IEP requirements

The IEP was modified under IDEA '97 to emphasize the involvement of students with special needs in a general education classroom setting with the services and modifications deemed necessary by the evaluation team.

The Present Levels of Educational Performance (PLEP) was changed to require a statement of how the child's disability affects his or her involvement and progress in the general curriculum. IDEA '97 established that there must be a connection between the special education and general education curricula. For this reason, the PLEP had to include an explanation of the extent to which the student will not be participating with nondisabled children in the general education class and in extracurricular and nonacademic activities.

The IEP now had an established connection to the general education setting. General education teachers were required to attend IEP meetings, and IEPs had to

> The 1997 reauthorization of IDEA made major changes in the areas of the evaluation procedures, parent rights, transition, and discipline.

> IDEA '97 established that there must be a connection between the special education and general education curricula.

provide the needed test accommodations that would be provided on all state- and district-wide assessments of the student with special needs. IDEA '97's emphasis on raising the standards of those in special education placed an additional requirement of a definitive reason why a standard general education assessment would not be deemed appropriate for a child and how the child should then be assessed.

Schools were required to assure that paraprofessionals who worked with students with disabilities received training relevant to their placement.

IDEA '97 looked at how parents were receiving annual evaluations on their child's IEP goals and determined that this was not sufficient feedback for parents; it then required schools to make reports to parents on the progress of their children at least as frequently as they reported on the progress of their nondisabled peers.

The IEP was also modified to include a review of the student's transitional needs and services specifically:

- Beginning as early as age fourteen for some activities (IDEA 2004 changed the maximum age for all activities to sixteen), and annually thereafter, the student's IEP must contain a statement of his or her transition service needs under the various components of that IEP that focus upon the student's courses of study (e.g., vocational education or advanced placement).

- Beginning at least one year before the student reaches the age of majority under state law, the IEP must contain a statement that the student has been informed of the rights under the law that will transfer to him or her upon reaching the age of majority.

Discipline

IDEA '97 broadened the schools' right to take a disciplinary action with children who have been classified as needing special education services and who knowingly possess or use illegal drugs or sell or solicit the sale of a controlled substance while at school or school functions.

Manifest determination review

Under IDEA '97, suspensions or disciplinary consequences could result in an alternative educational placement. This possibility was to be weighed by a manifest determination review, which is held by an IEP Team. Manifest determination reviews must occur no more than ten days after the disciplinary action. This review team has the sole responsibility of determining the following:

1. Does the child's disability impair his or her ability to understand the impact and consequences of the behavior under disciplinary action?

2. Did the child's disability impair the ability of the child to control the behavior subject to discipline?

Determination of the relationship between the student's disability and an inappropriate behavior could allow a change in placement to occur. However, other educational services specified in the IEP must continue in the new setting.

When no relationship between the inappropriate behavior and the disability is established, IDEA '97 used FAPE to allow that the relevant disciplinary procedures applicable to children without disabilities may be applied to the child with disabilities in the same manner in which they would be applied to children without disabilities.

Functional behavioral assessments (FBAs) and behavior intervention plans (BIPs) then became a requirement in many situations for schools to both modify and provide disciplinary consequences.

Finally, mediation was inserted as a new level of appeal before going to a hearing for disputes. States are required to pay for an impartial mediator to work to resolve disagreements with parents about the child's IEP or placement.

No Child Left Behind Act, PL 107-110 (2002)

NO CHILD LEFT BEHIND (NCLB), Public Law 107-110, was signed on January 8, 2002. It addresses accountability of school personnel for student achievement with the expectation that every child will demonstrate proficiency in reading, math, and science. The first full wave of accountability will be in twelve years when children who attended school under NCLB graduate, but the process to meet that accountability begins now. In fact, as students progress through the school system, testing will show if an individual teacher has effectively met the needs of the students. Through testing, each student's adequate yearly progress or lack thereof will be tracked.

NCLB affects regular and special education students, gifted students and slow learners, and children of every ethnicity, culture, and environment. NCLB is a document that encompasses every American educator and student.

Educators are affected as follows: elementary teachers (K–3) are responsible for teaching reading and using different, scientific-based approaches as needed; elementary teachers of upper grades will teach reading, math, and science; middle and high school teachers will teach to new, higher standards; sometimes, they will have to play catch-up with students who did not have adequate education in earlier grades.

NO CHILD LEFT BEHIND: addresses accountability of school personnel for student achievement with the expectation that every child will demonstrate proficiency in reading, math, and science

NCLB affects regular and special education students, gifted students and slow learners, and children of every ethnicity, culture, and environment. NCLB is a document that encompasses every American educator and student.

Special educators are responsible for teaching students to a level of proficiency comparable to that of their nondisabled peers. This requirement will raise the bar of academic expectations throughout the grades. For some students with disabilities, the criteria for getting a diploma will be more difficult. Although a small percentage of students with disabilities will need alternate assessment, they will still need to meet grade appropriate goals.

In order for special education teachers to meet the professional criteria of this act, they must be highly qualified, that is certified or licensed in their area of special education, and show proof of a specific level of professional development in the core subjects that they teach. As special education teachers receive specific education in the core subject they teach, they will be better prepared to teach to the same level of learning standards as the general education teacher.

IDEIA (IDEA 2004)

The second revision of IDEA occurred in 2004. IDEA was reauthorized as the Individuals with Disabilities Education Improvement Act of 2004 (IDEIA 2004), commonly referred to as IDEA 2004 (effective July 1, 2005).

The intention was to improve IDEA by adding the philosophy and understanding that special education students need preparation for further study beyond the high school setting-teaching compensatory methods. Accordingly, IDEA 2004 provided a close tie to PL 89-10, the Elementary and Special Education Act of 1965, and stated that students with special needs should have maximum access to the general curriculum. Maximum access was defined as the access required for an individual student to reach his fullest potential. Full inclusion was not to be the only option by which to achieve this, and the act specified that skills should be taught to compensate students later in life in cases where inclusion was not the best setting.

IDEA 2004 added a new requirement for special education teachers on the secondary level, enforcing NCLB's highly qualified requirements in the subject area of their curriculum. The rewording in this part of IDEA states that they shall be no less qualified than teachers in the core areas.

Free and Appropriate Public Education (FAPE) was revised by mandating that students have maximum access to appropriate general education. Additionally, LRE placement for those students with disabilities must have the same school placement rights as those students who do not have disabilities. IDEA 2004 recognizes that, because of the nature of some disabilities, appropriate education may vary in the amount of participation and placement in the general education setting. For some students, FAPE will mean a choice of the type of educational institution they attend (private school for example). Any such choice must provide the special education services deemed necessary for the student through the IEP.

The definition of assistive technology devices was amended to exclude devices that are surgically implanted (i.e., cochlear implants) and clarified that students with assistive technology devices shall not be prevented from having special education services. Assistive technology devices may need to monitored by school personnel, but schools are not responsible for the implantation or replacement of such devices surgically. An example of this would be a cochlear implant.

The definition of child with a disability as the term used for children ages 3–9 with a developmental delay was changed to allow inclusion of Tourette Syndrome.

IDEA 2004 recognized that all states must follow the *National Instructional Materials Accessibility Standards*, which states that students who need materials in a certain form will get those at the same time their nondisabled peers receive their materials. Teacher recognition of these standards is important.

Changes in requirements for evaluations

The time allowed between the request for an initial evaluation and the determination of whether a disability is present has been changed to state that the determination must occur within sixty calendar days of the request. This change is significant; previously, it was interpreted to mean sixty school days. Parental consent is also required for evaluations and before the start of special education services.

No single assessment or measurement tool may now be used to determine special education qualification. Assessments and measurements used should be in *language and form* that will give the most accurate picture of the child's abilities.

IDEA 2004 recognized that a disproportionate representation of minorities and bilingual students exist and that preservice interventions that are *scientifically based on early reading programs, positive behavioral interventions and support, and early intervening services* may mean that some of those children do not need special education services. This understanding has led to a child not being considered to have a disability if he or she has not had appropriate education in math or reading. In addition, a child is not considered to have a disability if the reason for the delays is that English is a second language.

When determining a specific learning disability, the criteria may use not only a discrepancy between a*chievement* and *intellectual ability*, but also whether or not the child responds to scientific research-based intervention. In general, children who may not have been found eligible for special education through testing but are known to need services (because of functioning, excluding lack of instruction) are still eligible for special education services. Because of this change, input for evaluation now includes state and local testing, classroom observation, academic achievement, and related developmental needs.

ELLs with Disabilities

Of growing concern to educators is the disproportionate rate of English language learners (ELLs) represented in classes of students with disabilities. Zehr (2001) reported that an estimated 184,000 of the nation's 2.9 million students (i.e., 6 percent) enrolled in programs for ELLs have disabilities, citing statistics from the U.S. Department of Education. Gurel (2004) reported that about 5 percent of the nation's school children have been identified with learning disabilities, though the percentage of ELLs has traditionally been higher over the years (Baca & Cervantes, 1989; Kretschmer, 1991 in Gurel, 2004).

The difficulty of accurate estimates stems from the fact that each state reports its ELLs who are served by special education differently (Robertson & Kushner, 1994 in Gurel, 2004). While it is true that the National Center for Educational Statistics (NCES); the No Child Left Behind Act (NCLB), 2002; and IDEA (1997) are all working to unify reporting criteria, there is still much work to be done in this area.

One way to serve the student with disabilities and the ELL student is to accurately assess their disability or limitation. How can teachers differentiate between ELLs with learning disabilities from those who are simply struggling with learning a second language? It is not easy. Many of the problems associated with second language learning are also identified as learning difficulties; for example, should processing difficulties, behavioral differences, reading difficulties, and expressive difficulties (Lock & Layton, 2002 in Gurel, 2004) be associated with the difficulties of second language learning or learning difficulties? While some learning difficulties can be partially identified by observation over a period of time or by a lack of academic improvement (Gersten & Baker, 2003 in Gurel, 2004), they are also typical of ELLs struggling with the complexities of language and a new school environment.

Therefore, it is of critical importance to assess the concerned student using a variety of testing procedures. Scribner & Scribner (2001 in Gurel 2004) recommend the prereferral team be composed of specialists from different disciplines, including a special educator and a bilingual educator. Other team members would be a school representative, a general educator, a family member, and a community member. An interpreter should be provided to the family member if needed. The report drawn up should include much the same information as required for special education referral: a statement of the problem, potential sources of the problem, relevant background information, and a written plan with a follow-up schedule (Litt, n.d., Markowitz et al.1997; Olson, 1991 in Gurel, 2004).

Suggestions to achieve an accurate testing procedure are:

- Tests that are nondiscriminatory based on race or culture

- Tests conducted in both the student's primary language and English

- Identify student using observations from school, home, and community

- Alternative assessments combined with formal assessments

- Criterion-referenced assessments

- Curriculum-based assessments

- Portfolio of student's work

- Informal assessments: rubrics, dynamic assessment (test-teach-test), learning logs, self-evaluations

- Comparison of student's cultural teaching style (e.g., teacher-centered) with the school's teaching style (e.g., student-centered)

Teaching strategies for ELLs with disabilities

For most students, regardless of the disability or lack of English, it is the general classroom teacher who is responsible for their learning (NCLB, 2002). ESL, bilingual, and special education have produced a wealth of techniques that can be used by all teachers to the benefit of their students. There is little research on the combined fields of English language learning with learning disabilities, yet there are many similarities in the recommended teaching strategies. Gurel (2004) has organized these strategies into before, during and after instruction recognizing that there may be overlapping within the processes. Suggestions to teachers are:

Before Instruction	Plan relevant curricula
	Plan for universal design
	Plan thematic units
	Align curricula across grades and subjects
	Implement the ESL standards
	Collaborate with other professionals
	Create a print-rich environment
	Set high expectations
	Teach at the appropriate difficulty
	Write clear objectives
	Build on student strengths

Continued on next page

During Instruction	Activate background knowledge
	Set students up to succeed
	Use active learning
	Use clinical teaching methods
	Teach in multiple modes
	Allow students to collaborate
	Use individual or small-group instruction
	Promote higher-order thinking skills
	Teach learning strategies
	Use graphic organizers
	Develop language in all content areas
	Focus on reading
	Incorporate technology
	Follow routines
	Provide clear instructions
After Instruction	Review frequently
	Use curriculum-based assessments
	Intervene at an early age
	Support the use of students' native language
	Extend the school year or offer summer school

Further reading on ELLs with disabilities

A major obstacle in working with ELLs with disabilities is the lack of guidelines dealing specifically with the two limitations. While both learning disabilities and teaching English to minorities or immigrants have been studied extensively, little research has been done on how to best integrate the two disciplines (Gersten & Baker, 2003; Ortiz, 1997 in Gurel 2004). The following suggestions for further reading are offered to those who seek more information.

- Aron, L.Y. & Loprest, P.J. (2007) *Meeting the Needs of Children with Disabilities*. Urban Institute Press.

- Echevarria, J. & Graves, A. (1998) *Sheltered Content Instruction: Teaching English-Language Learners with Diverse Abilities*. Allyn and Bacon.

- Gurel, Sarah M. (2004) *Teaching English Language Learners with Learning Disabilities: A Compiled Convergence of Strategies*. College of William and Mary. School of Education, Curriculum and Instruction.

- *http://learningdisabilities.about.com*

- *http://www.eric.ed.gov/*

- Zehr, Mary Ann (2008) "Bilingual Students with Disabilities Get Special Help." *Education Week*. Nov. 7, 2001. *http://www.edweek.org/ew/articles/2001/11/07/10clark.h21.html?print=1*

Changes in requirements for IEPs

Individualized Education Plans (IEPS) continue to have multiple sections. One section, *present levels of educational performance (PLEP)*, now addresses *academic achievement and functional performance*. Annual IEP goals must now address the same areas.

IEP goals should be aligned to state standards; therefore, short-term objectives are not required on every IEP. Students with IEPs must not only participate in regular education programs to the fullest extent possible, they must also show progress in those programs. Therefore, goals must be written to reflect academic progress.

For students who must participate in alternate assessment, there must be alignment to alternate achievement standards.

Significant change has been made in the definition of the IEP team. It now states that no less than one teacher from each of the areas of special education and regular education be present.

IDEA 2004 recognized that the amount of required paperwork placed upon teachers of students with disabilities should be reduced if possible. For this reason, some states will participate in a newly developed pilot program that uses multi-year IEPs. Individual student inclusion in this program will require consent by both the school and the parent.

SKILL 5.5 Major legislation

Significant Supreme Court Cases Involving Interpretation of IDEA

Following the passage of P.L. 94-142 and IDEA, questions have arisen over the interpretation of least restrictive environment and free, appropriate public education. The courts have been asked to judge the extent of a school district's obligation to provide support services and suspension procedures for students with disabilities. A brief description of some of the cases that the U.S. Supreme Court reviewed and the rulings are included in this section. These cases have addressed such issues as least restrictive environment, free and appropriate public education, transportation, suspension of exceptional education students, and provision of services in a private school setting.

Board of Education v. Rowley, 1982	This case concerned the interpretation of "Free and Public Education," and the lengths to which schools are required to go in order to provide it. Amy Rowley was a deaf elementary school student whose parents rejected their school district's proposal to provide a tutor and speech therapist services to supplement their daughter's instruction in the regular classroom. Her parents insisted on an interpreter, even though Amy was making satisfactory social, academic, and educational progress without one. They argued that although she was progressing well, there was a serious discrepancy between her level of achievement and her potential without the handicap. They held that the absence of an interpreter prevented her from reaching her full potential. In deciding in favor of the school district, the Supreme Court confirmed the act's requirement of a "basic floor of opportunity consistent with equal protection," but stated that this "basic floor" did not require "anything more than equal access." It explicitly ruled that schools are not required to "maximize the potential of handicapped children commensurate with the opportunity provided to other children." It further ruled that "if the child is being educated in the regular classrooms of the public education system, (services) should be reasonably calculated to enable the child to achieve passing marks and advance from grade to grade." Finally, the Court ruled that Amy did not need an interpreter, because "evidence firmly establishes that Amy is receiving an `adequate' education, since she performs better than the average child in her class and is advancing easily from grade to grade."
Irving Independent School District v. Tatro, 1984	IDEA lists health services as one of the related services that schools are mandated to provide to exceptional students. Amber Tatro, who had spina bifida, required the insertion of a catheter on a regular schedule in order to empty her bladder. The issue was specifically over the classification of clean, intermittent catheterization (CIC) as a medical service (not covered under IDEA) or a related health service, which would be covered. In this instance, the catheterization was not declared a medical service, but a related service necessary for the student to have in order to benefit from special education. The school district was obliged to provide the service. The Tatro case has implications for students with other medical impairments who may need services to allow them to attend classes at the school.
Smith v. Robinson, 1984	This case concerned reimbursement of attorney's fees for parents who win litigation under IDEA. At the time of this case, IDEA did not provide for such reimbursement. Following this ruling, Congress passed a law awarding attorney's fees to parents who win their litigation.
Honig v. Doe, 1988	Essentially, students may not be denied education or be excluded from school when their misbehavior is related to their handicap. The *stay put* provision of IDEA allows students to remain in their current educational setting pending the outcome of administrative or judicial hearings. In the case of behavior that is a danger to the student or others, the court allows school districts to apply their normal procedures for dealing with dangerous behavior, such as time-out, loss of privileges, detention, or study carrels. Where the student has presented an immediate threat to others, that student may be temporarily suspended for up to ten school days to give the school and the parents time to review the IEP and discuss possible alternatives to the current placement.

Table continued on next page

Oberti v. Board of Education of the Borough of Clementon School District, 1993	It was determined that IDEA requires school systems to supplement and realign their resources to move beyond those systems, structures, and practices that tend to result in unnecessary segregation of children with disabilities. The Act does *not* require states to offer *the same* educational experience to a child with disabilities as is generally provided for children without disabilities. To the contrary, states must address the unique needs of a disabled child, recognizing that that child may benefit differently from education in the regular classroom than other students. In summary, the fact that a child with disabilities will learn differently from his or her education within a regular classroom does not justify exclusion from that environment.
Brown v. Board of Education (1954)	While this case specifically addressed the inequality of separate but equal facilities on the basis of race, the concept that segregation was inherently unequal—even if facilities were provided—was later applied to handicapping conditions.
Pennsylvania Association for Retarded Citizens (PARC) v. Commonwealth of Pennsylvania (1972)	Special Education was guaranteed to children with mental retardation. The victory in this case sparked other court cases for children with other disabilities.
Mills v. Board of Education of the District of Columbia (1972)	The right to special education was extended to all children with disabilities, not just mentally retarded children. Judgments in PARC and Mills paved the way for P. L. 94-142.

SKILL 5.6 Roles and responsibilities of the special education teacher

When making eligibility, program, and placement decisions about a student, the special education teacher serves as a member of a multidisciplinary team. Teachers are involved in every aspect of the education of individual students; therefore, they need to be knowledgeable not only about teaching and instructional techniques, but also about support services. These services need to be coordinated, and teachers must be able to work in a collaborative manner.

Close contact and communication must be established and maintained between the school district staff, each base school, and the various specialists (or consultants) providing ancillary services. These persons often serve special needs students in auxiliary (e.g., providing help) and supplementary (e.g., in addition to) ways. Thus, the principles and methods of special education must be shared with regular educators, and tenets and practices of general education must be conveyed to special educators. Job roles and the unique responsibilities and duties of support specialists like speech/language therapists, physical and occupational therapists, social workers, school psychologists and nurses, and others need to be known by all teachers.

A system should be put into place for sharing program materials, tracking student mastery of goals and objectives, and supporting the various requirements of administrative and teaching staff. Because of the variety of learning objectives and the need to make the special education curriculum appropriate for each student, information sharing is critical.

Teaching consists of a multitude of roles. Teachers must plan and deliver instruction in a creative and innovative way so that students find learning both fun and intriguing. The teacher must also research various learning strategies, decide which to implement in the classroom, and balance that information according to the various learning styles and special needs of the students.

Simultaneously, the teacher must also observe for student learning, interactions, and on-task behavior while making mental or written notes regarding what is working in the lesson and how the students are receiving and using the information. This will provide the teacher with immediate feedback as to whether to continue with the lesson, slow the instruction, or present the lesson in another way. Teachers must also work collaboratively with other adults in the room and use them to maximize student learning. The teacher's job requires the teacher to establish a delicate balance among all these factors.

SKILL 5.7 Roles and responsibilities of other professionals who deliver special education services

Paraprofessionals and General Education Teachers

Paraprofessionals and general education teachers are also important collaborators with teachers of exceptional students. Although they may have daily exposure to exceptional students, they may not have the theoretical or practical experience to assure their effective interaction with such students. They do bring valuable perspective and opportunities for breadth and variety in an exceptional child's educational experience. General education teachers also offer curriculum and subject matter expertise and a high level of professional support, while paraprofessionals may provide insights born of their particular familiarity with individual students. CEC suggests that teachers can best collaborate with general education teachers and paraprofessionals by

- Offering information about the characteristics and needs of children with exceptional learning needs

- Discussing and brainstorming ways to integrate children with exceptionalities into various settings within the school community

- Modeling best practices and instructional techniques and accommodations and coaching others in their use

- Keeping communication about children with exceptional learning needs and their families confidential

- Consulting with these colleagues in the assessment of individuals with exceptional learning needs

- Engaging them in group problem-solving and in developing, executing, and assessing collaborative activities

- Offering support to paraprofessionals by observing their work with students and offering feedback and suggestions

Related Service Providers and Administrators

Related service providers and administrators offer specialized skills and abilities that are critical to the exceptional education teacher's ability to advocate for his or her student and meet a school's legal obligations to the student and his or her family. Related service providers—such as speech therapists, occupational therapists, and language therapists, psychologists, and physicians—offer expertise and resources unparalleled in meeting a child's developmental needs. Administrators are often experts in the resources available at the school and local education agency levels, as well as the culture and politics of a school system, and can be powerful partners in meeting the needs of exceptional education teachers and students.

A teacher's most effective approach to collaborating with these professionals includes the following:

- Confirming mutual understanding of the accepted goals and objectives of the student with exceptional learning needs as documented in his or her IEP

- Soliciting input about ways to support related service goals in classroom settings

- Understanding the needs and motivations of each professional and acting in support whenever possible

- Facilitating respectful and beneficial relationships between families and professionals

- Regularly and accurately communicating observations and data about the child's progress or challenges

Quite often, teachers have great success with involving families by just informing families of what is going on in the classroom. Newsletters are particularly effective at this. Parents love to know what is going on in the classroom. In newsletters, teachers can provide suggestions on how parents can help with the educational goals of the school. For example, teachers can recommend that parents read with their children for twenty minutes per day. To add effectiveness, teachers can also provide suggestions on what to do when their children come across difficult words or when they ask a question about comprehension. This gives parents practical strategies. In addition, when working with students with special needs, it is a good idea to give frequent updates on the student's progress.

Many IEPs require this of specific intervals. It is also helpful if a means (daily notebook, response sheet, etc.) is provided where parents can alert the teacher to issues at home that might impact the student (e.g., Johnny took his medication late or a change in home routine has upset him).

Professionals need to work together to ensure that students with disabilities receive the services outlined in the IEP. The speech/language pathologist, the occupational therapist, the general education teacher, and the special education teacher may all be providing services to one student. In order to ensure that the proper time is allotted for each service, the professionals involved will have to work together to develop a schedule for the student to ensure that nothing is left out and that all areas outlined in the IEP are addressed. This will also help to ensure that students with disabilities who can be taught in groups are grouped with other students who may have the same requirements. This can be effectively done only when professionals share schedules, student information, and student requirements. If they work together, they can accomplish a lot more than when working independently.

SKILL 5.8 Strengths and limitations of various collaborative approaches

Teachers of exceptional students are expected to manage many roles and respon-sibilities, not only concerning their students, but also with respect to students' caregivers and other educational, medical, therapeutic, and administrative professionals. Each professional should share information from his or her area of expertise with the team. For example, the child's previous teacher may be able to offer some suggestions about modifications that were previously successful, or the speech pathologist may have noticed an issue with background noise that would be relevant. The team should communicate often to verify the success or failure of the modifications and to adjust or add modifications as needed.

Teachers need to establish a working relationship with those they encounter in the classroom environment. There are six basic steps to having a rewarding collaborative working relationship, whether coworkers are paraprofessionals, aides, or volunteers. While it is understood that there are many titles for those who may be assisting in your room, this section will summarize their titles as "classroom assistants."

1. Get to know each other.

The best way to start a relationship with anyone is to find time alone to get to know each other. Give your new classroom assistant the utmost respect and look at this as an opportunity to share your talents and learn those of your coworker. Share what your strengths and weaknesses are, and listen to his or hers. This knowledge may create one of the best working relationships you have ever had.

2. Remember, communication is a two-way street.

This is especially important with your classroom assistant. Let him or her see you listening. Encourage him or her to ask for more information. Remember also that asking your classroom assistant for details and insights may help you further meet the needs of your students. It is also your responsibility to remove and prevent communication barriers in your working relationship. You are the professional! You must be the one to avoid giving negative criticism or put downs. Do not "read" motivations into the actions of your classroom assistant. Learn about him or her through communicating openly.

3. Establish clear roles and responsibilities.

Note that while the graph can be a useful starting place, it is often helpful to write out what roles and expectations you have for your classroom assistant together in a contract-type fashion.

4. Plan together.

Planning together lets your paraprofessionals know you consider them valuable; it also provides a timeline of expectations that will aid both of you in your classroom delivery to the students, and gives the impression to your students that you both know what is going to happen next.

Teachers of exceptional students are expected to manage many roles and responsibilities, not only concerning their students, but also with respect to students' caregivers and other educational, medical, therapeutic, and administrative professionals.

The Access Center for Improving Outcomes of All Students K-8 has defined these roles in a graph available at:

www.k8accesscenter .org/training_resources /documents /Tchr-ParaCollaboration.pdf

5. Show a united front.

It is essential to let your students know that both adults in the room deserve the same amount of respect. Have a plan in place on how you should address negative behaviors individually and together. DO NOT make a statement in front of your students that your classroom assistant is wrong. Take time to address issues you may have regarding class time privately, never in front of the class.

6. Reevaluate your relationship.

Feedback is wonderful! Stop every now and then and discuss how you are working as a team. Be willing to listen to suggestions. Taking this time may be your opportunity to improve your working relationship.

> *Learn more about Creating a Classroom Team:*
>
> *www.aft.org/pubs-reports /psrp/classroom_team.pdf*

Beyond Classroom Assistants: General Educators and Special Needs Educators Unite

According to IDEA 2004, students with disabilities are to participate in the general education program to the extent that it is beneficial for them. Because these students are included in a variety of general education activities and classes, the need for collaboration among teachers grows.

Co-teaching

> **CO-TEACHING:** both teachers actively teach in the general education classroom

One model that is used for general education and special education teachers to collaborate is CO-TEACHING. In this model, both teachers actively teach in the general education classroom. Perhaps both teachers will conduct a small science experiment group at the same time, switching groups at some point in the lesson. Perhaps in social studies, one teacher will lecture while the other teacher writes notes on the board or points out information on a map.

In the co-teaching model, the general education teacher and special needs educator often switch roles back and forth within a class period or perhaps at the end of a chapter or unit.

Push-in teaching

> **PUSH-IN TEACHING:** one type of differentiated instruction in which two teachers are teaching simultaneously

In the PUSH-IN TEACHING model, the special needs educator teaches parallel material in the general education classroom. When the regular education teacher teaches word problems in math, for example, the special needs educator may be working with some students on setting up the initial problems and having them complete the computation. Another example would be in science, when the general education teacher asks review questions for a test, and the special needs educator works with a student who has a review study sheet to show the answer from a group of choices.

In the push-in teaching model, it may appear that two versions of the same lesson are being taught, or that two types of student responses and activities are being monitored on the same material. The push-in teaching model is considered one type of differentiated instruction in which two teachers are teaching simultaneously.

Consultant teaching

In the **CONSULTANT TEACHING** model, the general education teacher conducts the class after planning with the special needs educator about how to differentiate activities so that the needs of the student with a disability are met.

For example, in a social studies classroom using the consultant teaching model, both teachers may discuss what the expectations will be for a student with a learning disability and fine motor difficulty when the class does reports on states. They may decide that doing a state report is appropriate for the student; however, the student may use a computer to write the report so that he or she can utilize the spell check feature and so that the work is legible.

Resource room or partial pull-out

The **RESOURCE ROOM** is a specialized instructional setting where students go for short periods of special work, to learn specific skills and behaviors in which the student is deficient. The student spends the remainder of the day in the regular classroom. Generally, the resource room is inside the school environment where the child goes to be taught by a teacher who is certified in the area of disability. The accommodations and services provided in the resource room are designed to provide the student access to an equal education in spite of his or her disability, and to help the student catch up and perform with his or her peers in the regular classroom. In this case, he or she returns to the regular classroom for other subjects because this is the Least Restrictive Environment (LRE). The resource room is usually a bridge to mainstreaming.

Resource room time should be scheduled so that the student does not miss academic instruction in his or her classroom or miss desirable nonacademic activities. For maximum effectiveness, the general education teacher and the special education teacher (in the resource room) collaborate on differentiating the student's activities so he or she can be integrated into the mainstream classroom.

Substantially separate classrooms

In some cases, a child's disability makes it impossible for him or her to succeed in a mainstream classroom. Some students might need very specialized forms of instruction not available in the general education class, or they may have emotional, attention, or medical difficulties that prevent them from accessing the

CONSULTANT TEACHING: the general education teacher conducts the class after planning with the special needs educator about how to differentiate activities so that the needs of the student with a disability are met

RESOURCE ROOM: a specialized instructional setting where students go for short periods of special work, to learn specific skills and behaviors in which the student is deficient

curriculum in a large group. For these students, a separate classroom where they receive their academic instruction is required. Special education teachers and, often, additional aides staff these classes and deliver specialized services.

Even in such a separate classroom, however, instructional collaboration between general education and special education teachers is very important. Children in these classrooms typically spend at least part of the day, for lunch, recess, enrichment, and social activities, etc., with a general education class. In order for transitions to move smoothly, teachers must coordinate times and activities. Often, the general education teacher will include the special education students in special projects where their work can be displayed with that of their grade peers. For example, when an entire grade level is doing display boards on dinosaurs or states, the special education teacher might modify the lesson so the students in the separate classroom produce a display, as well.

SKILL 5.9 Communication with stakeholders

Teachers of exceptional students are expected to manage many roles and responsibilities, not only as concern their students, but also with respect to students' caregivers and other involved educational, medical, therapeutic, and administrative professionals. Because the needs of exceptional students are by definition multidisciplinary, a teacher of exceptional children often serves as the hub of a many-pronged wheel, communicating, consulting, and collaborating with the various stakeholders in a child's educational life. Managing these relationships effectively can be a challenge, but it is central to successful work in exceptional education.

Because the needs of exceptional students are by definition multidisciplinary, a teacher of exceptional children often serves as the hub of a many-pronged wheel, communicating, consulting, and collaborating with the various stakeholders in a child's educational life. Managing these relationships effectively can be a challenge, but it is central to successful work in exceptional education.

Students

Useful standards developed by the Council for Exceptional Children (CEC) in 2003 outline best practices in communicating and relating to children and their families. For example, CEC guidelines suggest that effective teachers:

- Offer students a safe and supportive learning environment, including clearly expressed and reasonable expectations for behavior.

- Create learning environments that encourage self-advocacy and developmentally appropriate independence.

- Offer learning environments that promote active participation in independent or group activities.

Such an environment is an excellent foundation for building rapport and trust with students, and communicating a teacher's respect for and expectation that they take a measure of responsibility for their educational development. Ideally, mutual trust and respect will afford teachers opportunities to learn of and engage students' ideas, preferences, and abilities.

Effective Communication between Teachers and Families

Research proves that the more families are involved in a child's educational experience, the more that child will succeed academically. Families know students better than almost anyone and are a valuable resource for teachers of exceptional students. Often, an insight or observation from a family member or his or her reinforcement of school standards or activities means the difference between success and frustration in a teacher's work with children. Suggestions for relationship building and collaboration with parents and families include the following:

- Use laypersons' terms when communicating with families and make the communication available in the language of the home.

- Search out and engage family members' knowledge and skills in providing educational and therapeutic services to the student.

- Explore and discuss the concerns of families and help them find tactics for addressing those concerns.

- Plan collaborative meetings with children and their families and help them become active contributors to their educational team.

- Ensure that communications with and about families are confidential and conducted with respect for their privacy.

- Offer parents accurate and professionally presented information about the pedagogical and therapeutic work being done with their child. It is sometimes necessary to provide professional guidance about the child's disability or the techniques that will help. For example, the parent of a third grade child who reads at the first grade level checks out library books at the third grade level and insists that the child labor through trying to read them in the hope this will improve the child's reading skills. The teacher needs to explain that while it would be helpful for the parent to read that third grade level book to the child, books chosen for the child to read should be easy enough for the child to read about 95 percent of the text independently, even if this is below grade level. The teacher might help the parent find material that is age appropriate but written at the child's level.

- Keep parents abreast of their rights, of the kinds of practices that might violate their rights, and of available recourse if needed.

- Acknowledge and respect cultural differences.

One common difficulty occurs when teachers assume that involvement in education simply means that the parents show up to help at school events or participate in parental activities on campus. With this belief, many teachers devise clever strategies to increase parental involvement at school. However, just because a parent shows up to school and assists with an activity does not mean that the child will learn more. Many parents work all day long and cannot assist in the school. Teachers, therefore, have to think of different ways to encourage parental and family involvement in the educational process.

Parent Conferences

The parent-teacher conference is generally for one of three purposes. First, the teacher may wish to share information with the parents concerning the performance and behavior of the child. Second, the teacher may be interested in obtaining information from the parents about the child. Such information may help answer questions or concerns that the teacher has. A third purpose may be to request parent support or involvement in specific activities or requirements. In many situations, more than one of the purposes may be involved.

Planning the conference

When a conference is scheduled, whether at the request of the teacher or the parent, the teacher should allow sufficient time to prepare thoroughly. Collect all relevant information, samples of student work, records of behavior, and other items needed to help the parent understand the circumstances. It is also a good idea to compile a list of questions or concerns you wish to address. Arrange the time and location of the conference to provide privacy and to avoid interruptions.

Conducting the conference

Begin the conference by putting the parents at ease. Take the time to establish a comfortable mood, but do not waste time with unnecessary small talk. Begin your discussion with positive comments about the student. Identify strengths and desirable attributes, but do not exaggerate.

As you address issues or areas of concern, be sure to focus on observable behaviors and concrete results or information. Do not make judgmental statements about parent or child. Share specific work samples, anecdotal records of behavior, etc., that demonstrate clearly the concerns you have. Be a good listener and hear the parent's comments and explanations. Such background information can be invaluable in understanding the needs and motivations of the child.

Finally, end the conference with an agreed plan of action between parents and teacher (and, when appropriate, the child). Bring the conference to a close politely but firmly and thank the parents for their involvement.

After the conference

A day or two after the conference, it is a good idea to send a follow-up note to the parents. In this note, briefly and concisely reiterate the plan or step agreed to in the conference. Be polite and professional; avoid the temptation to be too informal or chatty. If the issue is a long term one such as the behavior or ongoing work performance of the student, make periodic follow-up contacts to keep the parents informed of the progress.

> ### SKILL 5.10 Potential bias issues that may impact teaching and interactions with students and their families

In providing services to students with disabilities and to their families, teachers need to be involved in a wide range of professional activities that will help improve their instruction and their effectiveness in the classroom. These should include self-reflection and self-assessment.

Self-reflection involves reflecting on one's practice to improve instruction and to guide professional growth. In the area of special education, this would entail evaluating how successful one is in ensuring that students are meeting their short- and long-term goals in the classroom. When teachers reflect on their own performance, they can evaluate what they are doing right and where improvements should be made.

The teacher should participate in professional activities and organizations that benefit individuals with exceptional needs, their families, and their colleagues. This will ensure that they are on the cutting edge of any new legislation that applies to special education teachers; it will also ensure that they are aware of the research-based best practices that are being implemented in teaching students with disabilities. They should incorporate the newly discovered research into their daily teaching practices.

Other activities that improve teacher effectiveness include using available and innovative resources and technologies to enhance personal productivity and efficiency; using methods to remain current regarding evidence-based practices; and maintaining student, familial, and collegial confidentiality.

Special education teachers needs to be aware of how personal cultural biases and differences impact one's teaching and learning. They should also be aware of professional organizations relevant to practice.

The self-assessment and reflection process should form the basis for decisions about programs and instructional strategies. After the teacher has reflected and assessed his or her own performance in the classroom, he or she should work to improve teaching practice, as professional growth is the practitioner's responsibility.

SAMPLE TEST

SAMPLE TEST

Development and Characteristics of Learners

(Skill 1.1) (Average)

1. Which behavior would be expected at the mild level of emotional/behavioral disorders?

   A. Attention-seeking

   B. Inappropriate affect

   C. Self-injurious

   D. Poor sense of identity

(Skill 1.1) (Average)

2. Short attention span, daydreaming, clumsiness, and preference for younger playmates are associated with:

   A. Conduct disorder

   B. Personality disorders

   C. Immaturity

   D. Socialized aggression

(Skill 1.1) (Rigorous)

3. Skilled readers use all but which one of these knowledge sources to construct meanings beyond the literal text?

   A. Text knowledge

   B. Syntactic knowledge

   C. Morphological knowledge

   D. Semantic knowledge

(Skill 1.1) (Rigorous)

4. Celia, who is in first grade, asked, "Where are my ball?" She also has trouble with passive sentences. Language interventions for Celia would target:

   A. Morphology

   B. Syntax

   C. Pragmatics

   D. Semantics

(Skill 1.1) (Rigorous)

5. Mr. Mendez is assessing his students' written expression. Which of these is not a component of written expression?

   A. Vocabulary

   B. Morphology

   C. Content

   D. Sentence structure

(Skill 1.1) (Easy)

6. A developmental delay may be indicated by:

   A. Second grader having difficulty buttoning clothing

   B. Stuttered response

   C. Kindergartner not having complete bladder control

   D. Withdrawn behavior

(Skill 1.1) (Average)

7. Which of the following best describes how different areas of development impact each other?

    A. Development in other areas cannot occur until cognitive development is complete.

    B. Areas of development are interrelated and impact each other.

    C. Development in each area is independent of development in other areas.

    D. Development in one area leads to a decline in other areas.

(Skill 1.1) (Easy)

8. Five-year-old Tom continues to substitute the "w" sound for the "r" sound when pronouncing words; therefore, he often distorts words (e.g., "wabbit" for "rabbit" and "wat" for "rat"). His articulation disorder is basically a problem in:

    A. Phonology

    B. Morphology

    C. Syntax

    D. Semantics

(Skill 1.1) (Easy)

9. Scott is in middle school but still makes statements like, "I gotted new high-tops yesterday," and "I saw three mans in the front office." Language interventions for Scott would target:

    A. Morphology

    B. Syntax

    C. Pragmatics

    D. Semantics

(Skill 1.2) (Average)

10. One common factor for students with all types of disabilities is that they are also likely to demonstrate difficulty with:

    A. Social skills

    B. Cognitive skills

    C. Problem-solving skills

    D. Decision-making skills

(Skill 1.2) (Average)

11. Amanda will not complete her assignment. She wants to control how it is done and when she will finish it. How can her teacher improve her motivation to do her work?

    A. Call her parent(s)

    B. Report to teachers and team members for suggestions

    C. Provide Amanda with a degree of choice

    D. Modify the assignment

(Skill 1.2) (Rigorous)

12. Alan has failed repeatedly in his academic work. He needs continuous feedback in order to experience small, incremental achievements. What type of instructional material would best meet this need?

    A. Programmed materials

    B. Audiotapes

    C. Materials with no writing required

    D. Worksheets

(Skill 1.3) (Easy)

13. Which is an educational characteristic common to students with mild intellectual learning and behavioral disabilities?

    A. Show interest in schoolwork

    B. Have intact listening skills

    C. Require modification in classroom instruction

    D. Respond better to passive than to active learning tasks

(Skill 1.5) (Rigorous)

14. Individuals with mild mental retardation can be characterized as:

    A. Often indistinguishable from normal developing children at an early age

    B. Having a higher than normal rate of motor activity

    C. Displaying significant discrepancies in ability levels

    D. Uneducable in academic skills

(Skill 1.5) (Rigorous)

15. David is a 16-year-old in your class who recently came from another country. The girls in your class have come to you to complain about the way he treats them in a sexist manner. When they complain, you reflect that this is also the way he treats adult females. You have talked to David before about appropriate behavior. You should first:

    A. Complain to the principal

    B. Ask for a parent-teacher conference

    C. Check to see if this is a cultural norm in his country

    D. Create a behavior contract for him to follow

(Skill 1.6) (Average)

16. Duration is an appropriate measure to take with all of these behaviors *EXCEPT*:

    A. Thumb sucking

    B. Hitting

    C. Temper tantrums

    D. Maintaining eye contact

(Skill 1.6) (Average)

17. All children cry, hit, fight, and play alone at different times. Children with behavior disorders will perform these behaviors at a higher than normal:

    A. Rate

    B. Topography

    C. Duration

    D. Magnitude

(Skill 1.6) (Rigorous)

18. Criteria for choosing behaviors that are most in need of change involve all of the following *EXCEPT*:

    A. Observations across settings to rule out certain interventions

    B. Pinpointing the behavior that is the poorest fit with the child's environment

    C. The teacher's concern about what is the most important behavior to target

    D. Analysis of the environmental reinforcers

(Skill 1.6) (Easy)

19. Marcie is often not in her seat when the bell rings. She may be found at the pencil sharpener, throwing paper away, or fumbling through her notebook. Which of these descriptions of her behavior can be described as a pinpoint?

    A. Is tardy

    B. Is out of seat

    C. Is not in seat when late bell rings

    D. Is disorganized

(Skill 1.7) (Easy)

20. Jacob's mother describes him as her "little leader." He organizes games at home, takes responsibility for setting the table, and initiates play. She states that her other, younger son is more of a follower; he is aloof and does not seem to stand up for himself. According to the Bowen theory, which factor may determine these differences between Jacob and his brother?

    A. Triangles

    B. Sibling position

    C. Nuclear family emotional system

    D. Family projection process

Planning and the Learning Environment

(Skill 2.1) (Easy)

21. A teacher can encourage student-directed instruction by providing:

    A. Learning centers

    B. Large group labs

    C. Textual resources

    D. Peer tutoring

(Skill 2.1) (Rigorous)

22. Methods of effectively presenting a lesson plan so it may reach a variety of learners include:

    A. Lecture

    B. Verbal reasoning

    C. Transparencies

    D. Audiovisual technology

(Skill 2.2) (Rigorous)

23. The Integrated approach to learning utilizes all resources available to address student needs. What are the resources?

    A. The student, his/her parents, and the teacher

    B. The teacher, the parents, and the special education team

    C. The teacher the student, and an administrator to perform needed interventions

    D. The student, his/her parents, the teacher and community resources

(Skill 2.2) (Rigorous)

24. Which of the following teaching activities is *LEAST* likely to enhance learning for students with special needs?

    A. A verbal description of the task to be performed, followed by having the children immediately attempt to perform the instructed behavior

    B. A demonstration of the behavior, followed by an immediate opportunity for the children to imitate the behavior

    C. A simultaneous demonstration and explanation of the behavior, followed by ample opportunity for the children to rehearse the instructed behavior

    D. Physically guiding the children through the behavior to be imitated, while verbally explaining the behavior

(Skill 2.4) (Average)

25. Multiple Intelligence Testing is supported by:

    A. IDEA research

    B. Brain-based research

    C. Educator trial and error

    D. All of the above

(Skill 2.4) (Rigorous)

26. Which is a less-than-ideal example of collaboration in successful inclusion?

    A. Special education teachers are part of the instructional team in a regular classroom

    B. Special education teachers are informed of the lesson beforehand and assist regular education teachers in the classroom

    C. Teaming approaches are used for problem solving and program implementation

    D. Regular teachers, special education teachers, and other specialists or support teachers co-teach

(Skill 2.4) (Average)

27. Bob was showing behavior problems such as lack of attentiveness, inability to remain seated, and talking out. His teacher has kept data on these behaviors and has found that Bob is showing much better self-control since he has been self-managing himself through a behavior modification program. The most appropriate placement recommendation for Bob at this time is probably:

    A. Any available part-time special education program

    B. The regular classroom, solely

    C. A behavior disorders resource room for one period per day

    D. A specific learning disabilities resource room for one period per day

(Skill 2.4) (Easy)

28. Educators who advocate educating all children, without exception, in their neighborhood classrooms and schools, who propose the end of labeling and segregation of special needs students in special classes, and who call for the delivery of special supports and services directly in the classroom may be said to support the:

    A. Full-service model

    B. Regular education initiative

    C. Full inclusion model

    D. Mainstream mode

(Skill 2.4) (Rigorous)

29. Shyquan is in your inclusive class, and she exhibits a slower comprehension of assigned tasks and concepts. Her first two grades were Bs but she is now receiving failing marks. She has seen the resource teacher. You should:

    A. Ask for a review of current placement

    B. Tell Shyquan to seek extra help

    C. Ask Shyquan if she is frustrated

    D. Ask the regular education teacher to slow instruction

(Skill 2.4) (Easy)

30. Howard Gardener suggests that students learn in at least:

    A. Eight ways

    B. Seven ways

    C. Six ways

    D. Eleven ways

(Skill 2.4) (Average)

31. What is the basis for the Inclusion Movement?

    A. ALL students belong in general education class—NO exception whatsoever.

    B. General education teachers can and should teach all students including those with disabilities.

    C. General education teachers will have all necessary supports to do this.

    D. All of the above

(Skill 2.5) (Average)

32. In a positive classroom environment, errors are viewed as:

    A. Symptoms of deficiencies

    B. Lack of attention or ability

    C. A natural part of the learning process

    D. The result of going too fast

(Skill 2.5) (Average)

33. Which of the following should be considered when planning the spatial arrangement of your classroom?

    A. Adequate physical space

    B. Lighting characteristics

    C. Window location

    D. All of the above

(Skill 2.5) (Average)

34. Appropriate safety features which should be used in learning environments with special needs students include:

    A. Physical barriers

    B. Effective procedures to be used in emergencies

    C. Equal treatment for all students to avoid stigma

    D. Multisensory instructional approach

(Skill 2.5) (Average)

35. Which of the following can be considered effective transitional strategies?

    A. Gathering materials during the planning stages of instruction rather than during instruction

    B. Keeping students informed of the sequencing of instructional activities

    C. Moving students in groups and clusters rather than one by one

    D. All of the above

(Skill 2.6) (Average)

36. In establishing a classroom behavior management plan with the students, it is best to:

    A. Have rules written and in place on day one

    B. Hand out a copy of the rules to the students on day one

    C. Have separate rules for each class on day one

    D. Have students involved in creating the rules on day one

(Skill 2.6) (Average)

37. Laura is beginning to raise her hand first instead of talking out. An effective schedule of reinforcement should be:

    A. Continuous

    B. Variable

    C. Intermittent

    D. Fixed

(Skill 2.6) (Easy)

38. Which of the following is *NOT* a feature of effective classroom rules?

    A. They are about four to six in number

    B. They are negatively stated

    C. Consequences are consistent and immediate

    D. They can be tailored to individual teaching goals and teaching styles

(Skill 2.6) (Average)

39. Instructional practices of the behavioral approach include which of the following?

    A. Use of concrete, hands-on materials

    B. Learning of abstract concepts

    C. Avoiding visual aids

    D. Conducting little error analysis

(Skill 2.6) (Average)

40. When developing a management plan, teachers must be:

    A. Focused on rewards systems

    B. Open to students dictating the rules

    C. Proactive

    D. Sole developer of rationale

(Skill 2.7) (Average)

41. Positive reinforcers are generally effective if they are desired by the student and:

    A. Worthwhile in size

    B. Given immediately after the desired behavior

    C. Given only upon the occurrence of the target behavior

    D. All of the above

(Skill 2.7) (Easy)

42. An effective classroom behavior management plan includes all but which of the following?

    A. Transition procedures for changing activities

    B. Clear consequences for rule infractions

    C. Concise teacher expectations for student behavior

    D. Copies of lesson plans

(Skill 2.7) (Rigorous)

43. Morgan frequently talks during instructional time. Her teacher, Mrs. Jenkins, wants to use the assertive discipline approach to behavior management to decrease, and eventually eliminate, Morgan's disruptions. All of the following interventions are appropriate *EXCEPT*:

    A. Offering Morgan positive reinforcement when she is quiet during instructional time

    B. Tracking Morgan's talk-outs and discussing them with her parents

    C. Promptly following through with expected consequences when Morgan talks out

    D. Focusing on the behavior and the situation rather than on Morgan's character

(Skill 2.7) (Easy)

44. Canter and Canter believe that behavior is:

    A. Uncontrollable

    B. Remote

    C. Innate

    D. Chosen

(Skill 2.7) (Average)

45. How can a teacher decide when rules are broken and complied with?

    A. A system of positive consequences, or rewards, can promote a positive classroom

    B. Positive expectations give the teacher an assertive response style

    C. Setting limits allows students to refrain from negative behavior

    D. All of the above

(Skill 2.7) (Rigorous)

46. The rule is "No talking during silent reading time." Mrs. Jenkins gives her students 20 minutes each Friday to quietly read a book or magazine of their choice. And every Friday, Karl turns to talk to Jake. What nonaversive technique may Mrs. Jenkins employ to reduce this undesirable behavior?

    A. Self-assessment

    B. Planned ignoring

    C. Proximity control

    D. Token economy

(Skill 2.8) (Easy)

47. Why should adequate lighting be considered for an exceptional student in the classroom?

    A. Full spectrum lighting should be available

    B. Fluorescent bulbs cause migraines

    C. Proper illumination is not critical

    D. Lighting provides a sense of atmosphere

(Skill 2.8) (Easy)

48. **Above all, the physical arrangement of the classroom must allow:**

    A. Safety measures

    B. Aesthetics

    C. Coloration

    D. Innovative technology

Instruction

(Skill 3.1) (Rigorous)

49. **What is the difference between an IFSP and an IEP?**

    A. An IFSP is created for children from birth to age three. An IEP is created for school-age children aged three to twenty-one.

    B. An IEP is created for children from birth to age three. An IFSP is created for school-age children aged three to twenty-one.

    C. An IFSP is not mandated by the IDEA whereas the IEP is mandated.

    D. An IEP is not mandated by the IDEA whereas the IFSP is mandated.

(Skill 3.1) (Rigorous)

50. **The minimum number of IEP meetings required per year is:**

    A. As many as necessary

    B. One

    C. Two

    D. Three

(Skill 3.2) (Average)

51. **What is an example of a cognitively demanding lesson?**

    A. A lesson that presents one piece of information

    B. A lesson with a single modality of teaching

    C. A lesson that requires the processing of three or four types of information

    D. A lesson broken into steps

(Skill 3.2) (Average)

52. **What is one way to differentiate the class in a large group setting?**

    A. Modify instruction time

    B. Avoid visual aids

    C. Do not allow breaks

    D. Establish a rule

(Skill 3.2) (Average)

53. **Who determines peer tutoring goals?**

    A. Peers

    B. IEP team

    C. Teachers

    D. Consultant teachers

(Skill 3.2) (Easy)

54. **What are organizers?**

    A. Learning tools

    B. Visual aids

    C. Diagrams

    D. All of the above

(Skill 3.3) (Average)

55. To facilitate learning instructional objectives:

    A. They should be taken from a grade-level spelling list

    B. They should be written and shared

    C. They should be arranged in order of similarity

    D. They should be taken from a scope and sequence

(Skill 3.3) (Average)

56. Which of the following is a good example of a generalization?

    A. Jim has learned to add and is now ready to subtract.

    B. Sarah adds sets of units to obtain a product.

    C. Bill recognizes a vocabulary word on a billboard when traveling.

    D. Jane can spell the word "net" backwards to get the word "ten."

(Skill 3.4) (Average)

57. In 2000, the National Reading Panel reviewed research on reading instruction showing that:

    A. Top-down approaches that emphasize meaning, like the whole-language approach, are the most effective reading programs

    B. Bottom-up or code-emphasis approaches like phonics are the most effective for reading programs

    C. There are five critical components of an effective reading program: phonemic awareness, phonics, fluency, vocabulary, and comprehension

    D. Approaches that emphasize sight word vocabulary and fluency are the most effective reading programs

(Skill 3.4) (Average)

58. What is the disadvantage of the whole-language method?

    A. The absence of writing

    B. The absence of phonics

    C. The exposure to print

    D. The use of language analysis

(Skill 3.4) (Average)

59. Marisol has been mainstreamed into a 9th grade language arts class. Although her behavior is satisfactory, and she likes the class, Marisol's reading level is about two years below grade level. The class has been assigned to read *Great Expectations* and to write a report. What intervention would be *LEAST* successful in helping Marisol complete this assignment?

    A. Having Marisol listen to a taped recording while following the story in the regular text

    B. Giving her a version of the story that is modified to her reading level

    C. Telling her to choose a different book that she can read

    D. Providing an abbreviated story outline at her reading level

(Skill 3.4) (Rigorous)

60. Mrs. Smith's students are engaged in activities such as saying rhyming words and words that begin with the same sound or finding pictures in a list that start with the same or different sound, changing the sounds in words (e.g., if 'dog' started with the same sound as 'cat' it would be 'cog'). There are no printed words or letters in the exercises. You can tell Mrs. Smith is trying to improve her students':

    A. Sight word recognition

    B. Phoneme awareness

    C. Vocabulary understanding

    D. Rreading comprehension

(Skill 3.4) (Average)

61. Teaching techniques that stimulate active participation and understanding in the mathematics class include *ALL BUT WHICH* of the following?

    A. Having students copy computation facts for a set number of times

    B. Allowing students extensive exploration and practice with manipulatives at a concrete level

    C. Giving students highlighters or post-it arrows for marking relevant information in problems

    D. Having both students and teacher model and talk aloud as they work through problems

(Skill 3.4) (Rigorous)

62. In what order does the National Council of Teachers of Mathematics (NCTM) say new math concepts and operations should be taught?

    A. Teach the meaning of symbols first, then pictures, then concrete manipulatives

    B. Teach with concrete manipulatives, then pictorial representations, then symbols

    C. Start with pictures, move to concrete manipulatives, then symbols and words

    D. Teach in any order as long as you do it consistently in all areas

(Skill 3.4) (Rigorous)

63. Although there are many strategies that can help students with disabilities learn new math concepts, what one strategy is almost universally necessary and helpful?

    A. More repetition of skills and practice problems

    B. More detailed teacher demonstrations of the concept

    C. More student time spent at the concrete level, interacting with manipulatives

    D. More homework practice on new concepts

(Skill 3.4) (Rigorous)

64. Kenny is a 9th grader enrolled in Wood Shop; he is having difficulty grasping fractions. You know that Kenny has difficulty with abstract concepts. What would be a good method to teach this concept?

  A. Pie blocks that proportionately measure whole, half, 1/4, 1/8, etc.

  B. Strips of paper that proportionately measure whole, half, 1/4, 1/8, etc.

  C. One-on-one review of the worksheet

  D. Working in the wood shop, privately showing him how to measure

(Skill 3.5) (Average)

65. For functional life problems, what can students ask themselves?

  A. What do I need in order to do the task? (Information needed to solve)

  B. What do I need to find out that I don't already know? (Relevant information)

  C. How can I find out what I need to know? (Strategy or plan)

  D. All of the above

(Skill 3.5) (Rigorous)

66. Functional curriculum focuses on all of the following *EXCEPT*:

  A. Skills needed for social living

  B. Occupational readiness

  C. Use of community resources

  D. Remedial academic skills

(Skill 3.6) (Easy)

67. What criteria must be considered when choosing assistive technology (AT) to help a particular student?

  A. Whether there is a specific need the AT can meet (e.g., a goal on the IEP that requires it)

  B. The degree of independence with which the student can use the device

  C. The need for collaborative planning for the device to be used across all relevant settings and transfer between settings

  D. All of the above

(Skill 3.6) (Easy)

68. John learns best through the auditory channel, so his teacher wants to reinforce his listening skills. Through which of the following types of equipment would instruction be most effectively presented?

  A. Overhead projector

  B. CD player

  C. Microcomputer

  D. Opaque projector

(Skill 3.6) (Average)

69. What Assistive Technology (AT) is best for Bob, who can compose well, but has difficulty with both encoding and the physical act of writing?

  A. A peer to write what he dictates

  B. Voice-to-text computer software

  C. A CD player he can listen to while others write

  D. A slant board for writing

(Skill 3.6) (Rigorous)

70. When a student begins to use assistive technology, it is important for the teacher to have a clear outline as to when and how the equipment should be used. Why?

    A. To establish a level of accountability with the student

    B. To establish that the teacher has responsibility for the equipment that is in use in his or her room

    C. To establish that the teacher is responsible for the usage of the assistive technology

    D. To establish a guideline for evaluation

(Skill 3.7) (Rigorous)

71. A transition or vocational curriculum approach focuses on:

    A. Remediation of basic academic skills

    B. Preparation for functioning in society as adults

    C. Preparation for the world of work

    D. Daily living and social skills

(Skill 3.7) (Average)

72. Transition planning for post-school life requires which of the following?

    A. School-based instruction tailored to meet the student's goals

    B. Community-based experiences for independent living or job skills

    C. Development of objectives related to specific employment and other post-school areas

    D. All of the above

(Skill 3.7) (Rigorous)

73. One of the most important goals of the special education teacher is to foster and create with the student:

    A. Handwriting skills

    B. Self-advocacy

    C. An increased level of reading

    D. Logical reasoning

(Skill 3.8) (Average)

74. All of the following are suggestions for pacing or altering the presentation of tasks to match the student's rate of learning *EXCEPT*:

    A. Teach in several shorter segments of time rather than a single lengthy session

    B. Continue to teach a task until the lesson is completed in order to provide more time on task

    C. Watch for nonverbal cues that indicate students are becoming confused, bored, or restless

    D. Avoid giving students an inappropriate amount of written work

(Skill 3.8) (Average)

75. How is student motivation increased when classroom instruction is modified?

    A. Students can manipulate materials that they use in their lives

    B. Students can practice new skills

    C. Students can process material easier

    D. Information is relevant to the student

(Skill 3.8) (Average)

76. **Why provide a student with a checklist or check sheet?**

    A. Students cannot track their accomplishments

    B. Check sheets are markers of success

    C. Checklists provide loose structure

    D. Check sheets relate material that is relevant to the student

Assessment

(Skill 4.1) (Rigorous)

77. **Which of the following purposes of testing calls for an informal test?**

    A. Screening a group of children to determine their readiness for the first reader

    B. Analyzing the responses of a student with a disability to various presentations of content material to see which strategy works for him

    C. Evaluating the effectiveness of a fourth-grade math program at the end of its first year of use in a specific school

    D. Determining the general level of intellectual functioning of a class of fifth graders

(Skill 4.1) (Easy)

78. **Stiggins' seven guiding principles for classroom assessment include:**

    A. Comprehensive procedures

    B. Appropriate targets

    C. Assessment judgments

    D. Proper usage

(Skill 4.1) (Average)

79. **What is a task through which a teacher can identify a student's metacognition?**

    A. Analysis of visual aids

    B. Reading a short text

    C. Demonstrating a word problem

    D. Using tactile materials

(Skill 4.1) (Average)

80. **What is the purpose of keeping student portfolios?**

    A. Compile student work

    B. Monitor progress over a period of time

    C. Presentation for parent-teacher conference

    D. All of the above

(Skill 4.2) (Average)

81. **Which of the following is *NOT* an appropriate assessment modification or accommodation for a student with a learning disability?**

    A. Having the test read orally to the student

    B. Writing down the student's dictated answers

    C. Allowing the student to take the assessment home to complete

    D. Extending the time for the student to take the assessment

(Skill 4.2) (Rigorous)

82. Formal assessments include standardized tests, norm-referenced instruments, and ____.

   A. developmental rating scales

   B. interviews

   C. anecdotes/observations

   D. textbook chapter tests

(Skill 4.2) (Easy)

83. Which of the following is an advantage of giving informal individual assessments, rather than standardized group tests?

   A. Questions can be modified to reveal a specific student's strategies or misconceptions

   B. The test administrator can clarify or rephrase questions for the student

   C. They can be inserted into the class quickly on an as needed basis

   D. All of the above

(Skill 4.2) (Rigorous)

84. Criterion-referenced tests can provide information about:

   A. Whether a student has mastered prerequisite skills

   B. Whether a student is ready to proceed to the next level of instruction

   C. Which instructional materials might be helpful in covering program objectives

   D. All of the above

(Skill 4.2) (Average)

85. Children who write poorly might be given tests that allow oral responses unless the purpose for the test is to:

   A. Assess handwriting skills

   B. Test for organization of thoughts

   C. Answer questions pertaining to math reasoning

   D. Assess rote memory

(Skill 4.2) (Easy)

86. The purpose of error analysis of a test is to:

   A. Determine what events were labeled in error

   B. Determine if the test length was the cause of error

   C. Evaluate the types of errors made by categorizing incorrect answers

   D. Establish a baseline

(Skill 4.2) (Rigorous)

87. The extent to which a test measures what it claims to measure is called:

   A. Reliability

   B. Validity

   C. Factor analysis

   D. Chi Square

(Skill 4.2) (Average)

88. **You are working with a functional program and have placed a student in a vocational position in the kitchen of a coffee house. A waiter takes orders and relays them to the student, whose job is to make the coffee as ordered. You need to perform a task analysis of making a cup of coffee. Which task should be first in the analysis?**

    A. Filling the pot with water

    B. Taking the order

    C. Measuring the coffee

    D. Picking the correct coffee

(Skill 4.3) (Average)

89. **How are informal assessments quantified and measured?**

    A. Via observational notes

    B. They cannot be quantified

    C. Decile scoring

    D. Percentile ranking

(Skill 4.3) (Easy)

90. **Standardized tests allow:**

    A. Administration to groups

    B. Administration to individuals

    C. Comparison across population

    D. All of the above

(Skill 4.3) (Average)

91. **What are individual intelligence tests primarily used for?**

    A. Program placement in a classroom

    B. Classification

    C. Defining a person's potential

    D. Screening groups

(Skill 4.3) (Average)

92. **Which components of the IEP are required by law?**

    A. Present level of academic and functional performance; statement of how the disability affects the student's involvement and progress; evaluation criteria and timelines for instructional objective achievement; modifications and accommodations

    B. Projected dates for services initiation with anticipated frequency, location, and duration; statement of when parent will be notified; statement of annual goals

    C. Extent to which child will not participate in regular education program; transitional needs for students age 14

    D. All of the above

(Skill 4.3) (Average)

93. **Which of the following words describes appropriate IEP objectives?**

    A. Specific

    B. Observable

    C. Measurable

    D. All of the above

(Skill 4.4) (Average)

94. In exceptional student education, assessment is used to make decisions about all of the following *EXCEPT:*

   A. Screening and initial identification of children who may need services

   B. Selection and evaluation of teaching strategies and programs

   C. Determining the desired attendance rate of a student

   D. Development of goals, objectives, and evaluation for the IEP

(Skill 4.4) (Average)

95. How can a diagnosis of readiness be assessed?

   A. Pretesting

   B. Multiple intelligences screening

   C. WISC

   D. Stanford-Binet

(Skill 4.4) (Average)

96. How do teachers make inferences in teaching methods?

   A. By gathering clues for student performance

   B. Meeting with the school psychologist

   C. Through instructional methods

   D. None of the above

Foundations and Professional Responsibilities

(Skill 5.1) (Average)

97. Which characteristic is not associated with autism?

   A. Engagement in repetitive activities or movements

   B. Resistance to environmental change or change in daily routine

   C. Unusual responses to sensory experiences

   D. Concomitant hearing and visual impairment

(Skill 5.1) (Rigorous)

98. Which of the following is typical of attention problems that a youngster with a learning disability might display?

   A. Lack of selective attention

   B. Does not consider consequences before acting

   C. Unable to control own actions or impulses

   D. Poor fine motor coordination

(Skill 5.1) (Average)

99. Echolalia, repetitive stereotyped actions, and a severe disorder of thinking and communication are indicative of:

   A. Psychosis

   B. Schizophrenia

   C. Autism

   D. Paranoia

(Skill 5.1) (Average)

100. In which of the following exceptionality categories may a student be considered for inclusion if his IQ score falls more than two standard deviations below the mean?

    A. Mental retardation

    B. Specific learning disabilities

    C. Emotionally/behaviorally disordered

    D. Gifted

(Skill 5.1) (Average)

101. According to IDEA 2004, students with disabilities are to do what?

    A. Participate in the general education program to the fullest extent that it is beneficial for them

    B. Participate in a vocational training within the general education setting

    C. Participate in a general education setting for physical education

    D. Participate in a Full Inclusion program that meets their needs

(Skill 5.1) (Average)

102. Which of the following are critical to the success of the exceptional student placed in a general education classroom?

    A. Access to appropriate accommodations and modifications

    B. Support from the special education teacher

    C. The general education teacher's belief that the student will profit from the placement

    D. All of the above

(Skill 5.1) (Easy)

103. Which of these groups is not comprehensively covered by IDEA?

    A. Gifted and talented

    B. Mentally retarded

    C. Specific learning disabilities

    D. Speech and language impaired

(Skill 5.1) (Average)

104. Michael's teacher complains that he is constantly out of his seat. She also reports that he has trouble paying attention to what is going on in class for more than a couple of minutes at a time. He appears to be trying, but his writing is often illegible, containing many reversals. Although he seems to want to please, he is very impulsive and stays in trouble with his teacher. He is failing reading, and his math grades, though somewhat better, are still below average. Michael's psychometric evaluation should include assessment for:

    A. Mild mental retardation

    B. Specific learning disabilities

    C. Mild behavior disorders

    D. Hearing impairment

(Skill 5.1) (Easy)

105. What is true about IDEA? In order to be eligible, a student must:

    A. Have a medical disability

    B. Have a disability that fits into one of the categories listed in the law

    C. Have a disability that actually affects school performance

    D. Both B and C

(Skill 5.1) (Average)

106. **Students with autistic tendencies can be more successful academically when the teacher:**

   A. Ignores inappropriate behaviors

   B. Allows them to go out of the room during instruction

   C. Keeps a calendar on the board of expected transitions

   D. Asks the CSE for a 1:1 aide

(Skill 5.2) (Average)

107. **What determines whether a person is entitled to protection under Section 504?**

   A. The individual must meet the definition of a person with a disability

   B. The person must be able to meet the requirements of a particular program in spite of his or her disability

   C. The school, business, or other facility must be the recipient of federal funding assistance

   D. All of the above

(Skill 5.5) (Average)

108. **How was the training of special education teachers changed by the No Child Left Behind Act of 2002?**

   A. It required all special education teachers to be certified in reading and math

   B. It required all special education teachers to take the same coursework as general education teachers

   C. If a special education teacher is teaching a core subject, he or she must meet the standard of a highly-qualified teacher in that subject

   D. All of the above

(Skill 5.6) (Easy)

109. **A consultant teacher should be meeting the needs of his/her students by:**

   A. Pushing in to do small group instruction with regular education students

   B. Reviewing lesson plan content for accuracy

   C. Meeting with the teacher before class to discuss adaptations and modifications

   D. Accompanying the student to class

(Skill 5.7) (Average)

110. **Which of the following is a responsibility that can *NOT* be delegated to a classroom aide?**

   A. Small group instruction

   B. Small group planning

   C. Designing a lesson plan

   D. Assist in BIP implementation

(Skill 5.7) (Rigorous)

111. **What can you do to create a good working environment with a classroom assistant?**

   A. Plan lessons with the assistant

   B. Write a contract that clearly defines his/her responsibilities in the classroom

   C. Remove previously given responsibilities

   D. All of the above

(Skill 5.7) (Average)

112. A paraprofessional has been assigned to assist you in the classroom. What action on the part of the teacher would lead to a poor working relationship?

A. Having the paraprofessional lead a small group

B. Telling the paraprofessional what you expect him/her to do

C. Defining classroom behavior management as your responsibility alone

D. Taking an active role in his/her evaluation

(Skill 5.7) (Rigorous)

113. Janice requires occupational therapy and speech therapy services. She is your student. What must you do to ensure her needs are met?

A. Watch the services being rendered

B. Schedule collaboratively

C. Ask for services to be given in a push-in model

D. Ask them to train you to give the service

(Skill 5.8) (Average)

114. The best way to ensure the success of educational interventions is to:

A. Give regular education teachers the primary responsibility of teaching special needs students in regular classrooms

B. Give special education teachers the primary responsibility of teaching special needs students in special education classrooms

C. Promote cooperative teaching efforts between general and special educators

D. Have support personnel assume the primary responsibility for the education of special needs students

(Skill 5.8) (Average)

115. A serious hindrance to successful mainstreaming is:

A. Lack of adapted materials

B. Lack of funding

C. Lack of communication among teachers

D. Lack of support from administration

(Skill 5.8) (Easy)

116. Jane is a third grader. Mrs. Smith, her teacher, noted that Jane was having difficulty with math and reading assignments. The results from recent diagnostic tests showed a strong sight vocabulary, strength in computational skills, but a weakness in comprehending what she read. This weakness was apparent in mathematical word problems as well. The multidisciplinary team recommended placement in a special education resource room for learning disabilities two periods each school day. For the remainder of the school day, her placement will be:

   A. In the regular classroom

   B. At a special school

   C. In a self-contained classroom

   D. In a resource room for mental retardation

(Skill 5.9) (Easy)

117. All of the following are essential components of effective parent-teacher conferences *EXCEPT*:

   A. Collecting samples of student work, records of behavior, and other relevant information

   B. Beginning the conference with positive comments about the student

   C. Using informal small talk to put the parents at ease

   D. Preparing a list of questions or concerns you wish to address

(Skill 5.9) (Average)

118. Parent contact should first begin when:

   A. You are informed the child will be your student

   B. The student fails a test

   C. The student exceeds others on a task

   D. An IEP meeting is scheduled and you have had no previous replies to letters

(Skill 5.9) (Average)

119. You should prepare for a parent-teacher conference by:

   A. Memorizing student progress/grades

   B. Anticipating questions

   C. Scheduling the meetings during your lunch time

   D. Planning a tour of the school

(Skill 5.9) (Rigorous)

120. Lotzie is not labeled as needing special education services, but he appears to be unable to function at his grade level both academically and socially. He is in 9th grade, but reads picture books and consistently displays immature behavior that can be misinterpreted. You have already observed these behaviors. What should be done first?

   A. Establish a rapport with the parents

   B. Write a CSE referral

   C. Plan and discuss possible interventions with the teacher

   D. Address the class about acceptance

Answer Key

ANSWER KEY							
1. A	16. B	31. D	46. C	61. A	76. B	91. B	106. C
2. C	17. A	32. C	47. A	62. B	77. B	92. D	107. D
3. C	18. C	33. D	48. A	63. C	78. B	93. D	108. C
4. B	19. C	34. B	49. A	64. B	79. A	94. C	109. C
5. B	20. B	35. D	50. B	65. D	80. D	95. A	110. C
6. A	21. A	36. D	51. C	66. D	81. C	96. A	111. A
7. B	22. D	37. A	52. A	67. D	82. D	97. D	112. C
8. A	23. D	38. B	53. C	68. B	83. D	98. A	113. B
9. A	24. A	39. A	54. D	69. B	84. A	99. C	114. C
10. A	25. B	40. C	55. C	70. A	85. A	100. A	115. C
11. C	26. B	41. D	56. C	71. B	86. C	101. A	116. A
12. A	27. B	42. D	57. C	72. D	87. B	102. D	117. C
13. C	28. C	43. B	58. B	73. B	88. D	103. A	118. A
14. A	29. A	44. D	59. C	74. B	89. A	104. B	119. B
15. C	30. B	45. D	60. B	75. A	90. D	105. D	120. A

Rigor Table

RIGOR TABLE	
Rigor level	**Questions**
Easy 25%	6, 8, 9, 13, 19, 20, 21, 28, 30, 38, 42, 44, 47, 48, 54, 67, 68, 78, 83, 86, 90, 103, 105, 109, 116, 117
Average Rigor 50%	1, 2, 7, 10, 11, 16, 17, 25, 27, 31, 32, 33, 34, 35, 36, 37, 39, 40, 41, 45, 51, 52, 53, 55, 56, 57, 58, 59, 61, 65, 69, 72, 74, 75, 76, 79, 80, 81, 85, 88, 89, 91, 92, 93, 94, 95, 96, 97, 99, 100, 101, 102, 104, 106, 107, 108, 110, 112, 114, 115, 118, 119
Rigorous 25%	3, 4, 5, 12, 14, 15, 18, 22, 23, 24, 26, 29, 43, 46, 49, 50, 60, 62, 63, 64, 66, 70, 71, 73, 77, 82, 84, 87, 98, 111, 113, 120

Sample Test with Rationales

Development and Characteristics of Learners

(Skill 1.1) (Average)

1. Which behavior would be expected at the mild level of emotional/behavioral disorders?

    A. Attention-seeking

    B. Inappropriate affect

    C. Self-injurious

    D. Poor sense of identity

    Answer: A. Attention-seeking

    Children who exhibit mild behavioral disorders are characterized by:

    - Average or above-average scores on intelligence tests
    - Poor academic achievement; learned helplessness
    - Unsatisfactory interpersonal relationships
    - Immaturity; attention seeking

(Skill 1.1) (Average)

2. Short attention span, daydreaming, clumsiness, and preference for younger playmates are associated with:

    A. Conduct disorder

    B. Personality disorders

    C. Immaturity

    D. Socialized aggression

    Answer: C. Immaturity

    These disorders show immaturity. The student is not acting age-appropriately.

(Skill 1.1) (Rigorous)

3. Skilled readers use all but which one of these knowledge sources to construct meanings beyond the literal text?

    A. Text knowledge

    B. Syntactic knowledge

    C. Morphological knowledge

    D. Semantic knowledge

    Answer: C. Morphological knowledge

    The student is already skilled, so morphological knowledge is already in place.

(Skill 1.1) (Rigorous)

4. Celia, who is in first grade, asked, "Where are my ball?" She also has trouble with passive sentences. Language interventions for Celia would target:

    A. Morphology

    B. Syntax

    C. Pragmatics

    D. Semantics

    Answer: B. Syntax

    Syntax refers to the rules for arranging words to make sentences.

(Skill 1.1) (Rigorous)

5. Mr. Mendez is assessing his students' written expression. Which of these is not a component of written expression?

   A. Vocabulary

   B. Morphology

   C. Content

   D. Sentence structure

Answer: B. Morphology

Morphology is correct. Vocabulary consists of words, content is made up of ideas, which are expressed in words, and sentences are constructed from words. Morphemes, however, are not always words. They may be prefixes or suffixes. Problems in this area would usually be considered problems with the mechanics of language, not expression.

(Skill 1.1) (Easy)

6. A developmental delay may be indicated by:

   A. Second grader having difficulty buttoning clothing

   B. Stuttered response

   C. Kindergartner not having complete bladder control

   D. Withdrawn behavior

Answer: A. Second grader having difficulty buttoning clothing

Buttoning clothing is generally mastered by the age of four. While many children have full bladder control by age four, it is not unusual for "embarrassing accidents" to occur.

(Skill 1.1) (Average)

7. Which of the following best describes how different areas of development impact each other?

   A. Development in other areas cannot occur until cognitive development is complete.

   B. Areas of development are interrelated and impact each other.

   C. Development in each area is independent of development in other areas.

   D. Development in one area leads to a decline in other areas.

Answer B. Areas of development are interrelated and impact each other.

Child development does not occur in a vacuum. Each element of development impacts other elements of development. For example, as cognitive development progresses, social development often follows. The reason for this is that all areas of development are fairly interrelated.

(Skill 1.1) (Easy)

8. Five-year-old Tom continues to substitute the "w" sound for the "r" sound when pronouncing words; therefore, he often distorts words (e.g., "wabbit" for "rabbit" and "wat" for "rat"). His articulation disorder is basically a problem in:

   A. Phonology

   B. Morphology

   C. Syntax

   D. Semantics

Answer: A. Phonology

Phonology refers to the study of the basic, individual sounds (phonemes) used in the language and the manner in which those individual sounds can be combined into words. Tom is substituting sounds so it is a problem in phonology. It may be related to a physiologically based articulation problem or to a hearing problem.

(Skill 1.1) (Easy)

9. Scott is in middle school but still makes statements like, "I gotted new high-tops yesterday," and "I saw three mans in the front office." Language interventions for Scott would target:

    A. Morphology

    B. Syntax

    C. Pragmatics

    D. Semantics

Answer A: Morphology

Morphology is the process of combining phonemes into meaningful words. It includes inflections and affixes related to tense and number.

(Skill 1.2) (Average)

10. One common factor for students with all types of disabilities is that they are also likely to demonstrate difficulty with:

    A. Social skills

    B. Cognitive skills

    C. Problem-solving skills

    D. Decision-making skills

Answer A: Social skills

Students with disabilities (in all areas) may demonstrate difficulty in social skills. For a student with a hearing impairment, social skills may be difficult because of not hearing social language. However, the emotionally disturbed student may have difficulty because of a special type of psychological disturbance.

(Skill 1.2) (Average)

11. Amanda will not complete her assignment. She wants to control how it is done and when she will finish it. How can her teacher improve her motivation to do her work?

    A. Call her parent(s)

    B. Report to teachers and team members for suggestions

    C. Provide Amanda with a degree of choice

    D. Modify the assignment

Answer: C. Provide Amanda with a degree of choice

Motivation may be improved by allowing the student a degree of choice in what is being taught or how it will be taught. Although asking fellow teachers for suggestions is also appropriate, Amanda may simply need to be motivated by having slight power over her assignment.

(Skill 1.2) (Rigorous)

12. **Alan has failed repeatedly in his academic work. He needs continuous feedback in order to experience small, incremental achievements. What type of instructional material would best meet this need?**

    A. Programmed materials

    B. Audiotapes

    C. Materials with no writing required

    D. Worksheets

    Answer: A. Programmed materials

    Programmed materials are best suited, as Alan would be able to chart his progress as he achieves each goal. He can monitor himself and take responsibility for his successes.

(Skill 1.3) (Easy)

13. **Which is an educational characteristic common to students with mild intellectual learning and behavioral disabilities?**

    A. Show interest in schoolwork

    B. Have intact listening skills

    C. Require modification in classroom instruction

    D. Respond better to passive than to active learning tasks

Answer: C. Require modification in classroom instruction

Some of the characteristics of students with mild learning and behavioral disabilities are as follows: Lack of interest in schoolwork; prefer concrete rather than abstract lessons; weak listening skills; low achievement; limited verbal and/ or writing skills; respond better to active rather than passive learning tasks; have areas of talent or ability often overlooked by teachers; prefer to receive special help in regular classroom; higher dropout rate than regular education students; achieve in accordance with teacher expectations; require modification in classroom instruction; and are easily distracted.

(Skill 1.5) (Rigorous)

14. **Individuals with mild mental retardation can be characterized as:**

    A. Often indistinguishable from normal developing children at an early age

    B. Having a higher than normal rate of motor activity

    C. Displaying significant discrepancies in ability levels

    D. Uneducable in academic skills

    Answer: A. Often indistinguishable from normal developing children at an early age

    See rationale of the previous question.

(Skill 1.5) (Rigorous)

15. David is a 16-year-old in your class who recently came from another country. The girls in your class have come to you to complain about the way he treats them in a sexist manner. When they complain, you reflect that this is also the way he treats adult females. You have talked to David before about appropriate behavior. You should first:

    A. Complain to the principal

    B. Ask for a parent-teacher conference

    C. Check to see if this is a cultural norm in his country

    D. Create a behavior contract for him to follow

    Answer: C. Check to see if this is a cultural norm in his country

    While A, B, and D are good actions, it is important to remember that David may come from a culture where woman are treated differently than they are here in America. Learning this information will enable the school as a whole to address this behavior. At that point it may be useful to talk to parents or involve a counselor in helping David learn how to adjust his behavior to meet new cultural norms. It might also involve class study of aspects of his culture that will be viewed as positive by his peers in order to improve his acceptance.

(Skill 1.6) (Average)

16. Duration is an appropriate measure to take with all of these behaviors *EXCEPT*:

    A. Thumb sucking

    B. Hitting

    C. Temper tantrums

    D. Maintaining eye contact

    Answer: B. Hitting

    Hitting takes place in an instant. This should be measured by frequency.

(Skill 1.6) (Average)

17. All children cry, hit, fight, and play alone at different times. Children with behavior disorders will perform these behaviors at a higher than normal:

    A. Rate

    B. Topography

    C. Duration

    D. Magnitude

    Answer: A. Rate

    Rate describes how often a behavior occurs.

(Skill 1.6) (Rigorous)

18. Criteria for choosing behaviors that are most in need of change involve all of the following *EXCEPT*:

    A. Observations across settings to rule out certain interventions

    B. Pinpointing the behavior that is the poorest fit with the child's environment

    C. The teacher's concern about what is the most important behavior to target

    D. Analysis of the environmental reinforcers

Answer C: The teacher's concern about what is the most important behavior to target

(Skill 1.6) (Easy)

19. Marcie is often not in her seat when the bell rings. She may be found at the pencil sharpener, throwing paper away, or fumbling through her notebook. Which of these descriptions of her behavior can be described as a pinpoint?

   A. Is tardy

   B. Is out of seat

   C. Is not in seat when late bell rings

   D. Is disorganized

   Answer: C. Is not in seat when late bell rings

   Even though A, B, and D describe the behavior, C is most precise. It is very objective (anyone can take the measurement) and pinpoints the exact behavior so it can be measured and altered. Once the behavior is pinpointed, it can be measured for the baseline phase of a behavior modification plan.

(Skill 1.7) (Easy)

20. Jacob's mother describes him as her "little leader." He organizes games at home, takes responsibility for setting the table, and initiates play. She states that her other, younger son is more of a follower; he is aloof and does not seem to stand up for himself. According to the Bowen theory, which factor may determine these differences between Jacob and his brother?

   A. Triangles

   B. Sibling position

   C. Nuclear family emotional system

   D. Family projection process

   Answer: B. Sibling position

   According to research, i.e., the Bowen theory, sibling position impacts family development. Older children tend to gravitate toward leadership positions, while younger children prefer to take a more passive, follower type of role. Although birth order is a propensity, it is not fixed. Though a teacher may encounter siblings during his or her career, it is imperative that the students are treated as individuals.

Planning and the Learning Environment

(Skill 2.1) (Easy)

21. A teacher can encourage student-directed instruction by providing:

   A. Learning centers

   B. Large group labs

   C. Textual resources

   D. Peer tutoring

Answer: A. Learning centers

Student-directed learning entails students making use of materials presented and learning among themselves. Students explore content independently. A learning center can provide tools necessary for autonomous exploration of a particular topic area.

(Skill 2.1) (Rigorous)

22. **Methods of effectively presenting a lesson plan so it may reach a variety of learners include:**

    A. Lecture

    B. Verbal reasoning

    C. Transparencies

    D. Audiovisual technology

Answer: D. Audiovisual technology

Coupled with hand-outs, graphic organizers, and general instruction, audiovisual modalities of presenting material via Smartboards, PowerPoint presentations, and the like activate various areas of the brain simultaneously, thus enhancing the learning experience for many students.

(Skill 2.2) (Rigorous)

23. **The Integrated approach to learning utilizes all resources available to address student needs. What are the resources?**

    A. The student, his/her parents, and the teacher

    B. The teacher, the parents, and the special education team

    C. The teacher the student, and an administrator to perform needed interventions

    D. The student, his/her parents, the teacher and community resources

Answer: D. The student, his/her parents, the teacher and community resources

The integrated response encompasses all possible resources including the resources in the community.

(Skill 2.2) (Rigorous)

24. **Which of the following teaching activities is *LEAST* likely to enhance learning for students with special needs?**

    A. A verbal description of the task to be performed, followed by having the children immediately attempt to perform the instructed behavior

    B. A demonstration of the behavior, followed by an immediate opportunity for the children to imitate the behavior

    C. A simultaneous demonstration and explanation of the behavior, followed by ample opportunity for the children to rehearse the instructed behavior

    D. Physically guiding the children through the behavior to be imitated, while verbally explaining the behavior

Answer: A. A verbal description of the task to be performed, followed by having the children immediately attempt to perform the instructed behavior

A verbal description alone does not give the students a chance to observe or see the behavior so that they can imitate it. Some of the students may have hearing deficiencies. In addition, students with special needs often benefit from hands-on, multi-modal activities.

(Skill 2.4) (Average)

25. **Multiple Intelligence Testing is supported by:**

    A. IDEA research

    B. Brain-based research

    C. Educator trial and error

    D. All of the above

    Answer: B. Brain-based research

    Brain-based learning suggests that knowledge is retained by the brain in ways that enable educators to design the most effective learning environments and maximize curriculum access.

(Skill 2.4) (Rigorous)

26. **Which is a less-than-ideal example of collaboration in successful inclusion?**

    A. Special education teachers are part of the instructional team in a regular classroom

    B. Special education teachers are informed of the lesson beforehand and assist regular education teachers in the classroom

    C. Teaming approaches are used for problem solving and program implementation

    D. Regular teachers, special education teachers, and other specialists or support teachers co-teach

    Answer: B. Special education teachers are informed of the lesson beforehand and assist regular education teachers in the classroom

    In an inclusive classroom, all students need to see both teachers as equals. This situation places the special education teacher in the role of a paraprofessional/teacher aide. Both teachers should be co-teaching in some way.

(Skill 2.4) (Average)

27. Bob was showing behavior problems such as lack of attentiveness, inability to remain seated, and talking out. His teacher has kept data on these behaviors and has found that Bob is showing much better self-control since he has been self-managing himself through a behavior modification program. The most appropriate placement recommendation for Bob at this time is probably:

    A. Any available part-time special education program

    B. The regular classroom, solely

    C. A behavior disorders resource room for one period per day

    D. A specific learning disabilities resource room for one period per day

    Answer: B. The regular classroom, solely

    Bob is able to self-manage himself and is very likely to behave like the other children in the regular classroom. The classroom is the least restrictive environment.

(Skill 2.4) (Easy)

28. Educators who advocate educating all children, without exception, in their neighborhood classrooms and schools, who propose the end of labeling and segregation of special needs students in special classes, and who call for the delivery of special supports and services directly in the classroom may be said to support the:

    A. Full-service model

    B. Regular education initiative

    C. Full inclusion model

    D. Mainstream mode

    Answer: C. Full inclusion model

    Advocates of Full Inclusion believe that all students must be included in the regular classroom, without exception.

(Skill 2.4) (Rigorous)

29. Shyquan is in your inclusive class, and she exhibits a slower comprehension of assigned tasks and concepts. Her first two grades were Bs but she is now receiving failing marks. She has seen the resource teacher. You should:

    A. Ask for a review of current placement

    B. Tell Shyquan to seek extra help

    C. Ask Shyquan if she is frustrated

    D. Ask the regular education teacher to slow instruction

    Answer: A. Ask for a review of current placement

    All of the responses listed above may be useful at one time or another, but you are responsible for reviewing her ability to function in the inclusive environment. Shyquan may or may not know she is not grasping the work, and she has sought out extra help with the resource teacher. If the regular education class students are successful, the class should not be slowed to adjust to Shyquan's learning rate. It is more likely that she may require a more modified curriculum to stay on task and to succeed academically. This might require a more restrictive environment, or at least more significant modifications and accommodations.

(Skill 2.4) (Easy)

30. **Howard Gardener suggests that students learn in at least:**

    A. Eight ways

    B. Seven ways

    C. Six ways

    D. Eleven ways

    Answer: B. Seven ways

    In 1999, Gardener suggested students learn in at least seven different ways, including visually/spatially, musically, verbally, logically/mathematically, interpersonally, intrapersonally, and bodily/kinesthetically.

(Skill 2.4) (Average)

31. **What is the basis for the Inclusion Movement?**

    A. ALL students belong in general education class—NO exception whatsoever.

    B. General education teachers can and should teach all students including those with disabilities.

    C. General education teachers will have all necessary supports to do this.

    D. All of the above

    Answer: D. All of the above

    The Inclusion Movement also reflects that quality education is a right, not a privilege. Success, literacy and graduation are a must for all students. Alternative channels will be created for students who cannot otherwise succeed.

(Skill 2.5) (Average)

32. **In a positive classroom environment, errors are viewed as:**

    A. Symptoms of deficiencies

    B. Lack of attention or ability

    C. A natural part of the learning process

    D. The result of going too fast

    Answer: C. A natural part of the learning process

    We often learn a great deal from our mistakes and shortcomings. It is normal. Where it is not normal, fear develops. This fear of failure inhibits children from working and achieving. Copying and other types of cheating result from this fear of failure. It is particularly important for students with disabilities to learn this principle. They probably have a history of feeling as though the emphasis has been on their errors rather than on their learning.

(Skill 2.5) (Average)

33. **Which of the following should be considered when planning the spatial arrangement of your classroom?**

    A. Adequate physical space

    B. Lighting characteristics

    C. Window location

    D. All of the above

Answer: D. All of the above

All of these factors help determine whether the room is "invitational." A classroom must have adequate physical space so students can conduct themselves comfortably. Some students are distracted by windows, doors, pencil sharpeners, etc. The space must be organized in a manner that makes it easier for students to carry out their daily tasks.

Adequate lighting is also important. Flickering lights can produce headaches in children with latent epilepsy, and some students are very sensitive to the glare from florescent lights and will need shades or desk lamps to compensate.

Ventilation and climate control are particularly relevant for students with Autism spectrum disorders, who may be extremely sensitive to odors, or students with asthma who react badly to dusty or stuffy rooms.

Warmer subdued colors contribute to students' concentration on task items. Neutral hues for coloration of walls, ceiling, and carpet or tile are generally used in classrooms so distraction because of classroom coloration may be minimized.

(Skill 2.5) (Average)

34. **Appropriate safety features which should be used in learning environments with special needs students include:**

    A. Physical barriers

    B. Effective procedures to be used in emergencies

    C. Equal treatment for all students to avoid stigma

    D. Multisensory instructional approach

Answer: B. Effective procedures to be used in emergencies

None of the other three choices is a safety feature.

(Skill 2.5) (Average)

35. **Which of the following can be considered effective transitional strategies?**

    A. Gathering materials during the planning stages of instruction rather than during instruction

    B. Keeping students informed of the sequencing of instructional activities

    C. Moving students in groups and clusters rather than one by one

    D. All of the above

Answer: D. All of the above

Effective teachers manage transitions from one activity to another in a systematic way through efficient management of instructional matter, sequencing of instructional activities, moving students in groups, and employing academic transition signals (utterances that indicate movement of the lesson from one topic or activity to another). These practices are particularly important for students with disabilities. They may need extra time for transitions, or more advanced warning, or even a physical signal such as a bell or light, to help them make the change.

(Skill 2.6) (Average)

36. **In establishing a classroom behavior management plan with the students, it is best to:**

    A. Have rules written and in place on day one

    B. Hand out a copy of the rules to the students on day one

    C. Have separate rules for each class on day one

    D. Have students involved in creating the rules on day one

    Answer: D. Have students involved in creating the rules on day one

    Rules are easier to follow when students not only know the reason they are in place, but also took part in creating them. It may be good to have a few rules prewritten and then to discuss if they cover all the rules the students have created. If not, it is possible you may want to modify your set of prewritten rules.

(Skill 2.6) (Average)

37. **Laura is beginning to raise her hand first instead of talking out. An effective schedule of reinforcement should be:**

    A. Continuous

    B. Variable

    C. Intermittent

    D. Fixed

    Answer: A. Continuous

    Note that the behavior is new. The pattern of reinforcement should not be variable, intermittent, or fixed. Continuous reinforcement is most effective at establishing new behaviors.

(Skill 2.6) (Easy)

38. **Which of the following is *NOT* a feature of effective classroom rules?**

    A. They are about four to six in number

    B. They are negatively stated

    C. Consequences are consistent and immediate

    D. They can be tailored to individual teaching goals and teaching styles

    Answer B: They are negatively stated

    Rules should be positively stated, and they should follow the other three features listed.

(Skill 2.6) (Average)

39. **Instructional practices of the behavioral approach include which of the following?**

    A. Use of concrete, hands-on materials

    B. Learning of abstract concepts

    C. Avoiding visual aids

    D. Conducting little error analysis

    Answer: A. Use of concrete, hands-on materials

    The behavioral approach appeared in the 1970s. It incorporated task analysis, sequential steps, tactile and hands-on materials, visual and auditory teaching aids, and the like.

(Skill 2.6) (Average)

40. **When developing a management plan, teachers must be:**

    A. Focused on rewards systems

    B. Open to students dictating the rules

    C. Proactive

    D. Sole developer of rationale

    Answer: C. Proactive

    Although student-produced rules are welcomed, positive procedures and behavior management techniques should also be shaped to curb possible problems, and to reflect what behaviors are expected of the class.

(Skill 2.7) (Average)

41. **Positive reinforcers are generally effective if they are desired by the student and:**

    A. Worthwhile in size

    B. Given immediately after the desired behavior

    C. Given only upon the occurrence of the target behavior

    D. All of the above

    Answer: D. All of the above

    Timing and quality of the reinforcer are key to encourage the individual to continue the targeted behavior.

(Skill 2.7) (Easy)

42. **An effective classroom behavior management plan includes all but which of the following?**

    A. Transition procedures for changing activities

    B. Clear consequences for rule infractions

    C. Concise teacher expectations for student behavior

    D. Copies of lesson plans

    Answer: D. Copies of lesson plans

    Effective classroom management includes transition procedures, clear consequences for rule infractions, and concise teacher expectations for student behavior. Lesson plans outline the classroom activities, schedule, and agenda.

(Skill 2.7) (Rigorous)

43. **Morgan frequently talks during instructional time. Her teacher, Mrs. Jenkins, wants to use the assertive discipline approach to behavior management to decrease, and eventually eliminate, Morgan's disruptions. All of the following interventions are appropriate EXCEPT:**

    A. Offering Morgan positive reinforcement when she is quiet during instructional time

    B. Tracking Morgan's talk-outs and discussing them with her parents

    C. Promptly following through with expected consequences when Morgan talks out

    D. Focusing on the behavior and the situation rather than on Morgan's character

Answer: B. Tracking Morgan's talk-outs and discussing them with her parents

Assertive discipline, developed by Canter and Canter, is an approach to classroom control that allows the teacher to constructively deal with misbehavior and maintain a supportive environment for the students. The assumptions behind assertive discipline are:

• Behavior is a choice.

• Consequences for not following rules are natural and logical, not a series of threats or punishments.

• Positive reinforcement occurs for desired behavior.

• The focus is on the behavior and the situation, not the student's character.

Mrs. Jenkins should provide opportunities for Morgan to reduce her talk-outs and use natural and logical consequences before involving Morgan's parents.

(Skill 2.7) (Easy)

44. **Canter and Canter believe that behavior is:**

   A. Uncontrollable

   B. Remote

   C. Innate

   D. Chosen

Answer: D. Chosen

The assertive discipline school of thought is the essence of choice: Students choose their behaviors. Positive reinforcement is given to those students who make educated choices.

(Skill 2.7) (Average)

45. **How can a teacher decide when rules are broken and complied with?**

   A. A system of positive consequences, or rewards, can promote a positive classroom

   B. Positive expectations give the teacher an assertive response style

   C. Setting limits allows students to refrain from negative behavior

   D. All of the above

Answer: D. All of the above

Teachers must have sense of control in the classroom. Merely making rules is not enough to reinforce classroom expectations. Systems of consequences and rewards, limits, and assertive response styles all contribute to the classroom agenda.

(Skill 2.7) (Rigorous)

46. **The rule is "No talking during silent reading time." Mrs. Jenkins gives her students 20 minutes each Friday to quietly read a book or magazine of their choice. And every Friday, Karl turns to talk to Jake. What nonaversive technique may Mrs. Jenkins employ to reduce this undesirable behavior?**

   A. Self-assessment

   B. Planned ignoring

   C. Proximity control

   D. Token economy

Answer: C. Proximity control

Mrs. Jenkins can reduce the talking simply by stepping in Karl's direction. This signal can inhibit the extraneous talking, and encourage Karl to be on task, and not distract Jake, or the other students who may need absolute silence to focus.

(Skill 2.8) (Easy)

47. **Why should adequate lighting be considered for an exceptional student in the classroom?**

    A. Full spectrum lighting should be available

    B. Fluorescent bulbs cause migraines

    C. Proper illumination is not critical

    D. Lighting provides a sense of atmosphere

    Answer: A. Full spectrum lighting should be available

    Always report any inadequacies in classroom illumination, since there are some students who may require full-spectrum lighting due to a visual impairment. The students need to have continuity in the learning environment.

(Skill 2.8) (Easy)

48. **Above all, the physical arrangement of the classroom must allow:**

    A. Safety measures

    B. Aesthetics

    C. Coloration

    D. Innovative technology

Answer: A. Safety measures

Adequate traffic flow must be provided for students. Students and teachers need to be able to safely circulate through the room. Student safety is of the utmost importance.

Instruction

(Skill 3.1) (Rigorous)

49. **What is the difference between an IFSP and an IEP?**

    A. An IFSP is created for children from birth to age three. An IEP is created for school-age children aged three to twenty-one.

    B. An IEP is created for children from birth to age three. An IFSP is created for school-age children aged three to twenty-one.

    C. An IFSP is not mandated by the IDEA whereas the IEP is mandated.

    D. An IEP is not mandated by the IDEA whereas the IFSP is mandated.

Answer: A. An IFSP is created for children from birth to age three. An IEP is created for school-age children aged three to twenty-one.

The IFSP (for children birth to age three) and the IEP (for school age children, age three to twenty-one) are both mandated by the IDEA. They are legal documents meant to summarize relevant assessments and diagnoses, determine needed services, and provide a structure for the implementation of those services. The IFSP focuses on a child's family as a whole in the context of daily life and preparation for school. The IEP forms the basis for special services and instruction in the educational setting.

(Skill 3.1) (Rigorous)

50. **The minimum number of IEP meetings required per year is:**

    A. As many as necessary

    B. One

    C. Two

    D. Three

Answer: B. One

P. L. 99-457 IDEA (1986) requires at least an annual IEP meeting.

(Skill 3.2) (Average)

51. **What is an example of a cognitively demanding lesson?**

    A. A lesson that presents one piece of information

    B. A lesson with a single modality of teaching

    C. A lesson that requires the processing of three or four types of information

    D. A lesson broken into steps

Answer: C. A lesson that requires the processing of three or four types of information

Cognitively demanding lessons are filled with knowledge that needs to be rapidly processed. This rapid succession is cognitively burdensome for some students with special needs. The teacher can break the lesson into smaller, discrete steps to make it easier to absorb.

(Skill 3.2) (Average)

52. **What is one way to differentiate the class in a large group setting?**

    A. Modify instruction time

    B. Avoid visual aids

    C. Do not allow breaks

    D. Establish a rule

Answer: A. Modify instruction time

Keep instruction shorter for first grade to seventh grade, ranging from five to fifteen minutes. Allow students to stretch to keep alert, and use lecture-pause routines. Always ask questions that involve all students.

(Skill 3.2) (Average)

53. **Who determines peer tutoring goals?**

    A. Peers

    B. IEP team

    C. Teachers

    D. Consultant teachers

    Answer: C. Teachers

    Although input from all choices is relevant, the teacher should determine the target goals and select the material to be presented. The teacher is also required to monitor progress and evaluate the sessions.

(Skill 3.2) (Easy)

54. **What are organizers?**

    A. Learning tools

    B. Visual aids

    C. Diagrams

    D. All of the above

    Answer: D. All of the above

    Visual aids, such as organizers or graphics, including diagrams, tables, charts, and guides, alert the students to the nature and content of the lesson.

(Skill 3.3) (Average)

55. **To facilitate learning instructional objectives:**

    A. They should be taken from a grade-level spelling list

    B. They should be written and shared

    C. They should be arranged in order of similarity

    D. They should be taken from a scope and sequence

Answer C: They should be arranged in order of similarity

To facilitate learning, instructional objectives should be arranged in order according to their patterns of similarity. Objectives involving similar responses should be closely sequenced; thus, the possibility for positive transfer is stressed.

(Skill 3.3) (Average)

56. **Which of the following is a good example of a generalization?**

    A. Jim has learned to add and is now ready to subtract.

    B. Sarah adds sets of units to obtain a product.

    C. Bill recognizes a vocabulary word on a billboard when traveling.

    D. Jane can spell the word "net" backwards to get the word "ten."

    Answer: C. Bill recognizes a vocabulary word on a billboard when traveling.

    Generalization is the occurrence of a learned behavior in the presence of a stimulus other than the one that produced the initial response. Students must be able to expand or transfer what is learned to other settings (e.g., reading to math word problems, resource room to regular classroom). Transfer of learning can be positive or negative. Positive transfer occurs when elements of what is learned on one task are also applicable to a new task, so the second task is easier to learn. Negative transfer occurs when elements of what was learned on one task interfere with what needs to be learned on a new task.

(Skill 3.4) (Average)

57. In 2000, the National Reading Panel reviewed research on reading instruction showing that:

   A. Top-down approaches that emphasize meaning, like the whole-language approach, are the most effective reading programs

   B. Bottom-up or code-emphasis approaches like phonics are the most effective for reading programs

   C. There are five critical components of an effective reading program: phonemic awareness, phonics, fluency, vocabulary, and comprehension

   D. Approaches that emphasize sight word vocabulary and fluency are the most effective reading programs

Answer: C. There are five critical components of an effective reading program: phonemic awareness, phonics, fluency, vocabulary, and comprehension

According to the National Reading Panel, research clearly shows that all five components are necessary for a successful program. They recommend that all components be present in a balanced fashion, and that educators evaluate their proposed approach to ensure it covers all areas. Approaches that lack an emphasis on one of the five critical areas should be modified to ensure all areas are well-integrated into the instruction.

(Skill 3.4) (Average)

58. What is the disadvantage of the whole-language method?

   A. The absence of writing

   B. The absence of phonics

   C. The exposure to print

   D. The use of language analysis

Answer: B. The absence of phonics

The language-experience approach and other whole-language methodologies unfortunately lack a phonics component. Teachers would need to add this missing component into the program in some way. In addition, there is no set method of evaluating student progress.

(Skill 3.4) (Average)

59. Marisol has been mainstreamed into a 9th grade language arts class. Although her behavior is satisfactory, and she likes the class, Marisol's reading level is about two years below grade level. The class has been assigned to read *Great Expectations* and to write a report. What intervention would be *LEAST* successful in helping Marisol complete this assignment?

   A. Having Marisol listen to a taped recording while following the story in the regular text

   B. Giving her a version of the story that is modified to her reading level

   C. Telling her to choose a different book that she can read

   D. Providing an abbreviated story outline at her reading level

Answer: C. Telling her to choose a different book that she can read

A, B, and D are positive accommodations that allow her to access the same curriculum as her classmates. C denies Marisol access to the same curriculum accessed by the other students and violates her rights.

(Skill 3.4) (Rigorous)

60. Mrs. Smith's students are engaged in activities such as saying rhyming words and words that begin with the same sound or finding pictures in a list that start with the same or different sound, changing the sounds in words (e.g., if 'dog' started with the same sound as 'cat' it would be 'cog'). There are no printed words or letters in the exercises. You can tell Mrs. Smith is trying to improve her students':

    A. Sight word recognition

    B. Phoneme awareness

    C. Vocabulary understanding

    D. Rreading comprehension

Answer: B. Phoneme awareness

These tasks help the students hear and understand that words are made up of distinct sounds (phonemes) that must be blended together. Unlike phonics exercises, which involve attaching sounds to letter symbols, phoneme awareness can be done orally, with no letters or text at all. It is a manipulation of sounds, not letters. It is one of the five critical components of an effective reading program.

(Skill 3.4) (Average)

61. Teaching techniques that stimulate active participation and understanding in the mathematics class include *ALL BUT WHICH* of the following?

    A. Having students copy computation facts for a set number of times

    B. Allowing students extensive exploration and practice with manipulatives at a concrete level

    C. Giving students highlighters or post-it arrows for marking relevant information in problems

    D. Having both students and teacher model and talk aloud as they work through problems

Answer: A. Having students copy computation facts for a set number of times

Copying does not stimulate participation or understanding. All the other methods are proven to help students with disabilities participate and master math concepts.

(Skill 3.4) (Rigorous)

62. In what order does the National Council of Teachers of Mathematics (NCTM) say new math concepts and operations should be taught?

    A. Teach the meaning of symbols first, then pictures, then concrete manipulatives

    B. Teach with concrete manipulatives, then pictorial representations, then symbols

    C. Start with pictures, move to concrete manipulatives, then symbols and words

    D. Teach in any order as long as you do it consistently in all areas

Answer: B. Teach with concrete manipulatives, then pictorial representations, then symbols

NCTM's review of the research and of the developmental order of math concepts clearly show the effectiveness of teaching math concepts and operations in this order:

- Concrete Representations: The extensive exploration and use of objects and manipulatives to discover and then demonstrate operations and relationships

- Pictorial Representations (semi-abstract): The use of concrete pictures of objects and actions often in the presence of the objects as discoveries and demonstrations are made

- Symbolic Representations (abstract): The use of symbols exclusively to conduct operations, explorations, and discoveries about math concepts

(Skill 3.4) (Rigorous)

63. **Although there are many strategies that can help students with disabilities learn new math concepts, what one strategy is almost universally necessary and helpful?**

    A. More repetition of skills and practice problems

    B. More detailed teacher demonstrations of the concept

    C. More student time spent at the concrete level, interacting with manipulatives

    D. More homework practice on new concepts

Answer: C. More student time spent at the concrete level, interacting with manipulatives

Although specific strategies will depend upon the individual child's strengths and disability, more time spent allowing the student to interact with and to carry out operations with manipulatives and more time using manipulatives to illustrate concepts will almost universally be helpful. In addition, once moving to the next level (pictorial representations), it may be helpful to keep manipulatives near the pictures longer, as well.

(Skill 3.4) (Rigorous)

64. **Kenny is a 9th grader enrolled in Wood Shop; he is having difficulty grasping fractions. You know that Kenny has difficulty with abstract concepts. What would be a good method to teach this concept?**

    A. Pie blocks that proportionately measure whole, half, 1/4, 1/8, etc.

    B. Strips of paper that proportionately measure whole, half, 1/4, 1/8, etc.

    C. One-on-one review of the worksheet

    D. Working in the wood shop, privately showing him how to measure

Answer: B. Strips of paper that proportionately measure whole, half, 1/4, 1/8, etc.

Strips of paper can be used to teach the concept by tearing a whole sheet into proportionate pieces. They can also be used like a tape measure to measure a length of wood. Although other methods might help him learn the concept, this method of using a linear form will make generalization to the wood shop most likely.

(Skill 3.5) (Average)

65. **For functional life problems, what can students ask themselves?**

    A. What do I need in order to do the task? (Information needed to solve)

    B. What do I need to find out that I don't already know? (Relevant information)

    C. How can I find out what I need to know? (Strategy or plan)

    D. All of the above

    Answer: D. All of the above

    By asking such questions, students are able to solve the problem or make a decision. Then they can check to see if the decision or solution actually obtains what was desired.

(Skill 3.5) (Rigorous)

66. **Functional curriculum focuses on all of the following *EXCEPT*:**

    A. Skills needed for social living

    B. Occupational readiness

    C. Use of community resources

    D. Remedial academic skills

    Answer: D. Remedial academic skills

    Remedial academics may be applied but are not a focus. The primary goal is to achieve skills for functioning in society on an independent basis, where possible.

(Skill 3.6) (Easy)

67. **What criteria must be considered when choosing assistive technology (AT) to help a particular student?**

    A. Whether there is a specific need the AT can meet (e.g., a goal on the IEP that requires it)

    B. The degree of independence with which the student can use the device

    C. The need for collaborative planning for the device to be used across all relevant settings and transfer between settings

    D. All of the above

    Answer: D. All of the above

    In addition to the above, it is also necessary to consider the amount of training the student and staff will need with the device, the specific contexts in which the device will be used (e.g., a language board might be used in all settings, but a computer program might be used only in writing), and the plan for transitions and storage.

(Skill 3.6) (Easy)

68. **John learns best through the auditory channel, so his teacher wants to reinforce his listening skills. Through which of the following types of equipment would instruction be most effectively presented?**

    A. Overhead projector

    B. CD player

    C. Microcomputer

    D. Opaque projector

Answer: B. CD player

As he is an auditory learner, the ability to listen to information would help sharpen and further develop John's listening skills.

(Skill 3.6) (Average)

69. **What Assistive Technology (AT) is best for Bob, who can compose well, but has difficulty with both encoding and the physical act of writing?**

    A. A peer to write what he dictates

    B. Voice-to-text computer software

    C. A CD player he can listen to while others write

    D. A slant board for writing

Answer: B. Voice-to-text computer software

Voice- to-text computer software is ideal for a student who can compose well (written expression), but who cannot write down his thoughts either because he cannot encode (spell) adequately or because he has a physical disability that makes the physical act of writing difficult. The computer allows him to focus on his expression without worrying about physical mechanics. Dictating to a teacher or a peer will also work, but these are not forms of AT. Listening to a CD while others write is not access to the curriculum.

(Skill 3.6) (Rigorous)

70. **When a student begins to use assistive technology, it is important for the teacher to have a clear outline as to when and how the equipment should be used. Why?**

    A. To establish a level of accountability with the student

    B. To establish that the teacher has responsibility for the equipment that is in use in his or her room

    C. To establish that the teacher is responsible for the usage of the assistive technology

    D. To establish a guideline for evaluation

Answer: A. To establish a level of accountability with the student

Establishing clear parameters as to the usage of assistive technology in a classroom creates a level of accountability in the student. The student will know that the teacher understands the intended purpose and appropriate use of the device and expects the student to do so, as well.

(Skill 3.7) (Rigorous)

71. **A transition or vocational curriculum approach focuses on:**

    A. Remediation of basic academic skills

    B. Preparation for functioning in society as adults

    C. Preparation for the world of work

    D. Daily living and social skills

Answer: B. Preparation for functioning in society as adults

A transition or vocational curriculum approach focuses upon what students need to learn that will be useful to them and prepare them for functioning in society as adults. Life preparation includes not only occupational readiness, but also personal-social and daily living skills.

(Skill 3.7) (Average)

72. **Transition planning for post-school life requires which of the following?**

    A. School-based instruction tailored to meet the student's goals

    B. Community-based experiences for independent living or job skills

    C. Development of objectives related to specific employment and other post-school areas

    D. All of the above

Answer: D. All of the above

All of these are mandated by IDEA unless the CSE can provide evidence that they are unnecessary. Community-referenced instruction refers to instruction that takes place in the classroom but is designed to generalize to life outside the classroom. To do this, instruction will be designed to be as similar to the real-life community or home situation as possible (e.g., using checkbook registers obtained from banks to learn to balance a checkbook in class or watching a video on how to get on and off a city bus).

(Skill 3.7) (Rigorous)

73. **One of the most important goals of the special education teacher is to foster and create with the student:**

    A. Handwriting skills

    B. Self-advocacy

    C. An increased level of reading

    D. Logical reasoning

Answer B: Self-advocacy

When a student achieves the ability to recognize his or her deficits and knows how to correctly advocate for his or her needs, the child has learned one of the most important life skills. This is true regardless of the child's level of reading or reasoning ability. Many children with severe disabilities can be taught to ask for the help they need and to understand they have rights.

(Skill 3.8) (Average)

74. **All of the following are suggestions for pacing or altering the presentation of tasks to match the student's rate of learning EXCEPT:**

    A. Teach in several shorter segments of time rather than a single lengthy session

    B. Continue to teach a task until the lesson is completed in order to provide more time on task

    C. Watch for nonverbal cues that indicate students are becoming confused, bored, or restless

    D. Avoid giving students an inappropriate amount of written work

Answer: B. Continue to teach a task until the lesson is completed in order to provide more time on task

This action does not alter the subject content; neither does it alter the rate at which tasks are presented. Pacing is the term used for altering tasks to match the student's rate of learning. This can be done in two ways: altering the subject content and the rate at which tasks are presented. However, both methods require adjusting presentation based on the child's performance along the way, and introducing a new task only when the student has demonstrated mastery of the previous task in the learning hierarchy.

(Skill 3.8) (Average)

75. **How is student motivation increased when classroom instruction is modified?**

    A. Students can manipulate materials that they use in their lives

    B. Students can practice new skills

    C. Students can process material easier

    D. Information is relevant to the student

Answer: A. Students can manipulate materials that they use in their lives

Active learning experiences teach concepts that motivate students. The students can manipulate, weigh, measure, read, or write using materials and skills that relate to their daily lives.

(Skill 3.8) (Average)

76. **Why provide a student with a checklist or check sheet?**

    A. Students cannot track their accomplishments

    B. Check sheets are markers of success

    C. Checklists provide loose structure

    D. Check sheets relate material that is relevant to the student

Answer: B. Checklists are markers of success

Students with learning problems need frequent reinforcement for their efforts. Charts, graphs, and check sheets provide tangible markers of student achievement.

Assessment

(Skill 4.1) (Rigorous)

77. **Which of the following purposes of testing calls for an informal test?**

    A. Screening a group of children to determine their readiness for the first reader

    B. Analyzing the responses of a student with a disability to various presentations of content material to see which strategy works for him

    C. Evaluating the effectiveness of a fourth-grade math program at the end of its first year of use in a specific school

    D. Determining the general level of intellectual functioning of a class of fifth graders

Answer: B. Analyzing the responses of a student with disability to various presentations of content material to see which strategy works for him

Formal tests such as standardized tests or textbook quizzes are objective tests that include primarily questions for which there is only one correct answer. Some are teacher-prepared, but they are often commercially prepared and frequently standardized. To analyze the response of a student to types of presentation, informal methods such as observation or questioning are more useful.

(Skill 4.1) (Easy)
78. **Stiggins' seven guiding principles for classroom assessment include:**

    A. Comprehensive procedures

    B. Appropriate targets

    C. Assessment judgments

    D. Proper usage

    Answer: B. Appropriate targets

    Stiggins concludes that clear and appropriate targets are essential for classroom assessment.

(Skill 4.1) (Average)
79. **What is a task through which a teacher can identify a student's metacognition?**

    A. Analysis of visual aids

    B. Reading a short text

    C. Demonstrating a word problem

    D. Using tactile materials

Answer: A. Analysis of visual aids

When a student analyzes visual aids, a teacher can identify whether the student is using background knowledge to infer and predict information presented in the visual aid. Metacognition allows the student to clarify information as well.

(Skill 4.1) (Average)
80. **What is the purpose of keeping student portfolios?**

    A. Compile student work

    B. Monitor progress over a period of time

    C. Presentation for parent-teacher conference

    D. All of the above

Answer: D. All of the above

Student portfolios provide a wealth of information, as well as insight into the student's progress in a particular subject. They serve as great assessment tools and show samples of the student's understanding of various topics.

(Skill 4.2) (Average)
81. **Which of the following is *NOT* an appropriate assessment modification or accommodation for a student with a learning disability?**

    A. Having the test read orally to the student

    B. Writing down the student's dictated answers

    C. Allowing the student to take the assessment home to complete

    D. Extending the time for the student to take the assessment

Answer: C: Allowing the student to take the assessment home to complete

Unless a student is homebound, the student should take assessments in class or in another classroom setting. All the other items listed are appropriate accommodations.

(Skill 4.2) (Rigorous)

82. **Formal assessments include standardized tests, norm-referenced instruments, and _____.**

    A. developmental rating scales

    B. interviews

    C. anecdotes/observations

    D. textbook chapter tests

Answer: D. textbook chapter tests

Formal assessments are assessments such as standardized tests or textbook quizzes; objective tests that include primarily questions for which there is only one correct, easily identifiable answer. These can be commercial or teacher made assessments. Informal assessments have less objective measures, and may include anecdotes or observations that may or may not be quantified, interviews, informal questioning during a task, etc.

(Skill 4.2) (Easy)

83. **Which of the following is an advantage of giving informal individual assessments, rather than standardized group tests?**

    A. Questions can be modified to reveal a specific student's strategies or misconceptions

    B. The test administrator can clarify or rephrase questions for the student

    C. They can be inserted into the class quickly on an as needed basis

    D. All of the above

Answer: D. All of the above

Standardized group tests are administered to a group in a specifically prescribed manner, with strict rules to keep procedures, scoring, and interpretation of results uniform in all cases. Such tests allow comparisons to be made across populations, ages or grades. Informal assessments have less objective measures, and may include anecdotes or observations that may or may not be quantified, interviews, informal questioning during a task, etc. An example of an informal individually administered assessment might be watching a student sort objects to see what attribute is most important to the student, or questioning a student to see what he or she found confusing about a task.

(Skill 4.2) (Rigorous)

84. **Criterion-referenced tests can provide information about:**

    A. Whether a student has mastered prerequisite skills

    B. Whether a student is ready to proceed to the next level of instruction

    C. Which instructional materials might be helpful in covering program objectives

    D. All of the above

    Answer: A. Whether a student has mastered prerequisite skills

    In criterion-referenced testing, the emphasis is on assessing specific and relevant skills or knowledge bases that have been mastered. Items on criterion-referenced tests are often linked directly to specific instructional objectives.

(Skill 4.2) (Average)

85. **Children who write poorly might be given tests that allow oral responses unless the purpose for the test is to:**

    A. Assess handwriting skills

    B. Test for organization of thoughts

    C. Answer questions pertaining to math reasoning

    D. Assess rote memory

    Answer A: Assess handwriting skills

    It is necessary to have the child write if a teacher is assessing his or her skill in that domain.

(Skill 4.2) (Easy)

86. **The purpose of error analysis of a test is to:**

    A. Determine what events were labeled in error

    B. Determine if the test length was the cause of error

    C. Evaluate the types of errors made by categorizing incorrect answers

    D. Establish a baseline

    Answer: C. Evaluate the types of errors made by categorizing incorrect answers

    Error analysis examines how and why a person makes a mistake. In an informal reading inventory, for example, questions are given to specifically address possible errors. A math assessment might provide a selection of answers on a multiple-choice test that pinpoint whether the error is because of failure to understand place value, failure to regroup, or failure to remember basic addition facts, etc. Other tests that utilize error analysis provide specific possible answers to denote which error was made. The purpose of both is to see where problems lie and to provide clues to assist the learning process.

(Skill 4.2) (Rigorous)

87. **The extent to which a test measures what it claims to measure is called:**

    A. Reliability

    B. Validity

    C. Factor analysis

    D. Chi Square

Answer: B. Validity

Validity is defined as the degree to which a test measures is what it claims to measure. There are several kids of validity, such as content validity, construct validity, and predictive validity.

(Skill 4.2) (Average)

88. **You are working with a functional program and have placed a student in a vocational position in the kitchen of a coffee house. A waiter takes orders and relays them to the student, whose job is to make the coffee as ordered. You need to perform a task analysis of making a cup of coffee. Which task should be first in the analysis?**

    A. Filling the pot with water

    B. Taking the order

    C. Measuring the coffee

    D. Picking the correct coffee

Answer: D. Picking the correct coffee

While the student is in a coffee house, the task is to make coffee, not to wait on customers. There are different kinds of coffee (decaffeinated, regular, etc.) and they all have their appropriate canisters. The student must be able to choose the correct coffee before measuring it.

(Skill 4.3) (Average)

89. **How are informal assessments quantified and measured?**

    A. Via observational notes

    B. They cannot be quantified

    C. Decile scoring

    D. Percentile ranking

Answer: A. Via observational notes

At times informal assessments often do not have to be quantified if they can be easily scored. Anecdotal records and observational logs can be filled out, and interviewing or informal questioning is an efficient way to record results.

(Skill 4.3) (Easy)

90. **Standardized tests allow:**

    A. Administration to groups

    B. Administration to individuals

    C. Comparison across population

    D. All of the above

Answer: D. All of the above

Standardized tests are flexible and allow several types of comparisons to be made. Comparisons across populations, ages, genders, grades, and so forth can be made.

(Skill 4.3) (Average)

91. **What are individual intelligence tests primarily used for?**

    A. Program placement in a classroom

    B. Classification

    C. Defining a person's potential

    D. Screening groups

Answer: B. Classification

Individual intelligence tests are used to classify individuals. Often results are reflected in IEPs and similar legal documents to demonstrate the intelligence level of the individual. Newer types of testing are being put into practice, such as Howard Gardener's Multiple Intelligences.

(Skill 4.3) (Average)

92. **Which components of the IEP are required by law?**

    A. Present level of academic and functional performance; statement of how the disability affects the student's involvement and progress; evaluation criteria and timelines for instructional objective achievement; modifications and accommodations

    B. Projected dates for services initiation with anticipated frequency, location, and duration; statement of when parent will be notified; statement of annual goals

    C. Extent to which child will not participate in regular education program; transitional needs for students age 14

    D. All of the above

    Answer: D. All of the above

    IEPs must contain many elements and these are sometimes altered when legislation is updated or reauthorized, so educators must keep themselves apprised of the changes and amendments to laws.

(Skill 4.3) (Average)

93. **Which of the following words describes appropriate IEP objectives?**

    A. Specific

    B. Observable

    C. Measurable

    D. All of the above

Answer D: All of the above

All objectives in an Individual Education Plan should be specific, observable, and measurable. If they are not observable and measurable, it will be impossible to determine whether they have been met. If they are vague and nonspecific the same difficulty applies.

(Skill 4.4) (Average)

94. **In exceptional student education, assessment is used to make decisions about all of the following *EXCEPT*:**

    A. Screening and initial identification of children who may need services

    B. Selection and evaluation of teaching strategies and programs

    C. Determining the desired attendance rate of a student

    D. Development of goals, objectives, and evaluation for the IEP

    Answer C: Determining the desired attendance rate of a student

    School attendance is required, and assessment is not necessary to measure a child's attendance rate.

(Skill 4.4) (Average)

95. **How can a diagnosis of readiness be assessed?**

    A. Pretesting

    B. Multiple intelligences screening

    C. WISC

    D. Stanford-Binet

Answer: A. Pretesting

Providing a pretest, checklist, and making teacher observations identifies students who are not ready for new instruction. It also can identify any knowledge gaps.

(Skill 4.4) (Average)

96. **How do teachers make inferences in teaching methods?**

    A. By gathering clues for student performance

    B. Meeting with the school psychologist

    C. Through instructional methods

    D. None of the above

    Answer: A. By gathering clues for student performance

    When a teacher observes student performance, teachers can assess data to inform and impact strategies and instructional practices.

Foundations and Professional Responsibilities

(Skill 5.1) (Average)

97. **Which characteristic is not associated with autism?**

    A. Engagement in repetitive activities or movements

    B. Resistance to environmental change or change in daily routine

    C. Unusual responses to sensory experiences

    D. Concomitant hearing and visual impairment

Answer: D. Concomitant hearing and visual impairment

Autism is a developmental disability significantly affecting verbal and nonverbal communication and social interaction, generally evident before age three, that adversely affects a child's education performance. A, B, and C are characteristics often associated with autism.

(Skill 5.1) (Rigorous)

98. **Which of the following is typical of attention problems that a youngster with a learning disability might display?**

    A. Lack of selective attention

    B. Does not consider consequences before acting

    C. Unable to control own actions or impulses

    D. Poor fine motor coordination

Answer: A. Lack of selective attention

Here are some of the characteristics of persons with learning disabilities: Disorder in one or more basic psychological processes involved in understanding or in using spoken or written language that manifests itself in an imperfect ability to listen, think, speak, read, write, spell, or to do mathematical calculations. They cannot be attributed to visual, hearing, physical, intellectual, or emotional handicaps, or cultural, environmental, or economic disadvantage.

(Skill 5.1) (Average)

99. Echolalia, repetitive stereotyped actions, and a severe disorder of thinking and communication are indicative of:

A. Psychosis

B. Schizophrenia

C. Autism

D. Paranoia

Answer: C. Autism

The behaviors listed are indicative of autism.

(Skill 5.1) (Average)

100. In which of the following exceptionality categories may a student be considered for inclusion if his IQ score falls more than two standard deviations below the mean?

A. Mental retardation

B. Specific learning disabilities

C. Emotionally/behaviorally disordered

D. Gifted

Answer: A. Mental Retardation

Only about 1 to 1.5% of the population fit the AAMD's definition of mental retardation. They exhibit significantly sub-average general intellectual functioning with deficits in adaptive behavior, manifested during the developmental period, and adversely affecting educational performance.

(Skill 5.1) (Average)

101. According to IDEA 2004, students with disabilities are to do what?

A. Participate in the general education program to the fullest extent that it is beneficial for them

B. Participate in a vocational training within the general education setting

C. Participate in a general education setting for physical education

D. Participate in a Full Inclusion program that meets their needs

Answer: A. Participate in the general education program to the fullest extent that it is beneficial for them

The term "full inclusion" is not used in IDEA or federal statutes. IDEA requires that students be included in the least restrictive environment that meets their needs. It states that this should be as close to that experienced by students without disabilities as practical, but also states that not all students can benefit from full participation in general education classrooms, and school systems must provide for all levels of placement. This can mean that a particular student's LRE may restrict him/her to a substantially separate program for the entire school day, but it should be possible to meet most students' needs in a less restrictive setting. Choices B, C, and D are all examples of possible settings related to participating in the general education setting to the fullest extent possible.

(Skill 5.1) (Average)

102. **Which of the following are critical to the success of the exceptional student placed in a general education classroom?**

    A. Access to appropriate accommodations and modifications

    B. Support from the special education teacher

    C. The general education teacher's belief that the student will profit from the placement

    D. All of the above

    Answer D: All of the above

    In order for the exceptional student to be successful in the general education classroom, the needed curriculum and instructional accommodations and modifications must be made, and support from special education resources provided.

(Skill 5.1) (Easy)

103. **Which of these groups is not comprehensively covered by IDEA?**

    A. Gifted and talented

    B. Mentally retarded

    C. Specific learning disabilities

    D. Speech and language impaired

    Answer: A. Gifted and talented

    IDEA does not cover all exceptional children; it covers children with disabilities. The Gifted and Talented Children's Act (Public Law 95-56), of 1978 established guidelines for services to students who are gifted or talented.

(Skill 5.1) (Average)

104. **Michael's teacher complains that he is constantly out of his seat. She also reports that he has trouble paying attention to what is going on in class for more than a couple of minutes at a time. He appears to be trying, but his writing is often illegible, containing many reversals. Although he seems to want to please, he is very impulsive and stays in trouble with his teacher. He is failing reading, and his math grades, though somewhat better, are still below average. Michael's psychometric evaluation should include assessment for:**

    A. Mild mental retardation

    B. Specific learning disabilities

    C. Mild behavior disorders

    D. Hearing impairment

    Answer: B. Specific learning disabilities

    The definition of "learning disability" is "a disorder in one or more of the basic psychological processes involved in understanding or in using language, spoken or written." Tests need to show a discrepancy between potential and performance in order to indicate a specific learning disability. Classroom observations and samples of student work (such as impaired reading ability) also provide indicators of possible learning disabilities.

(Skill 5.1) (Easy)

105. What is true about IDEA? In order to be eligible, a student must:

A. Have a medical disability

B. Have a disability that fits into one of the categories listed in the law

C. Have a disability that actually affects school performance

D. Both B and C

Answer: D. Both B and C. Have a disability that fits into one of the categories listed in the law and affects school performance

Having a disability is not enough to warrant eligibility for special services. The disability must be shown to negatively impact school performance. In other words, it must prevent the student from accessing the curriculum all other students can access in some way.

(Skill 5.1) (Average)

106. Students with autistic tendencies can be more successful academically when the teacher:

A. Ignores inappropriate behaviors

B. Allows them to go out of the room during instruction

C. Keeps a calendar on the board of expected transitions

D. Asks the CSE for a 1:1 aide

Answer: C. Keeps a calendar on the board of expected transitions

Students with autism tend to demonstrate an inability to transition unless that transition is already expected. Placing calendars and a schedule where they can be seen is important.

(Skill 5.2) (Average)

107. What determines whether a person is entitled to protection under Section 504?

A. The individual must meet the definition of a person with a disability

B. The person must be able to meet the requirements of a particular program in spite of his or her disability

C. The school, business, or other facility must be the recipient of federal funding assistance

D. All of the above

Answer: D. All of the above

To be entitled to protection under Section 504, an individual must meet the definition of a person with a disability, which is: any person who (i) has a physical or mental impairment which substantially limits one or more of that person's major life activities, such as self-care, walking, seeing, breathing, working, and or learning; (ii) has a record of such impairment; or (iii) is regarded as having such an impairment.

(Skill 5.5) (Average)

108. **How was the training of special education teachers changed by the No Child Left Behind Act of 2002?**

A. It required all special education teachers to be certified in reading and math

B. It required all special education teachers to take the same coursework as general education teachers

C. If a special education teacher is teaching a core subject, he or she must meet the standard of a highly-qualified teacher in that subject

D. All of the above

Answer: C. If a special education teacher is teaching a core subject, he or she must meet the standard of a highly-qualified teacher in that subject

In order for special education teachers to be a student's sole teacher of a core subject, they must meet the professional criteria of NCLB. They must be highly qualified, that is, certified or licensed in their area of special education, and show proof of a specific level of professional development in the core subjects that they teach. As special education teachers received specific education in the core subject they teach, they will be prepared to teach to the same level of learning standards as the general education teacher.

(Skill 5.6) (Easy)

109. **A consultant teacher should be meeting the needs of his/her students by:**

A. Pushing in to do small group instruction with regular education students

B. Reviewing lesson plan content for accuracy

C. Meeting with the teacher before class to discuss adaptations and modifications

D. Accompanying the student to class

Answer: C. Meeting with the teacher before class to discuss adaptations and expectations

Students who receive consult services are receiving minimal services. They may require some modification to their educational programs, and a consultant teacher can help the mainstream teacher determine ways to differentiate instruction to meet the needs of the student, or to apply whatever accommodations are in the IEP. The regular education teacher is responsible for the content, not the consultant teacher. In a push-in model, the special education teacher comes into the classroom and teaches one or more students with special needs a differentiated form of the lesson the general education teacher is teaching the rest of the class.

(Skill 5.7) (Average)

110. **Which of the following is a responsibility that can *NOT* be delegated to a classroom aide?**

A. Small group instruction

B. Small group planning

C. Designing a lesson plan

D. Assist in BIP implementation

Answer: C. Designing a lesson plan

Teachers are responsible for all lesson planning. However, it can be helpful to encourage input from a good classroom aide who may notice something that would be useful to you in designing the plans.

(Skill 5.7) (Rigorous)

111. **What can you do to create a good working environment with a classroom assistant?**

    A. Plan lessons with the assistant

    B. Write a contract that clearly defines his/her responsibilities in the classroom

    C. Remove previously given responsibilities

    D. All of the above

Answer: A. Plan lessons with the assistant

Planning with your classroom assistant shows that you respect his/her input and allows you to see where he/she feels confident.

(Skill 5.7) (Average)

112. **A paraprofessional has been assigned to assist you in the classroom. What action on the part of the teacher would lead to a poor working relationship?**

    A. Having the paraprofessional lead a small group

    B. Telling the paraprofessional what you expect him/her to do

    C. Defining classroom behavior management as your responsibility alone

    D. Taking an active role in his/her evaluation

Answer: C. Defining classroom behavior management as your responsibility alone

When you do not allow another adult in the room to enforce the class rules, you create an environment where the other adult is seen as someone not to be respected. No one wants to be in a work environment where they do not feel respected.

(Skill 5.7) (Rigorous)

113. **Janice requires occupational therapy and speech therapy services. She is your student. What must you do to ensure her needs are met?**

    A. Watch the services being rendered

    B. Schedule collaboratively

    C. Ask for services to be given in a push-in model

    D. Ask them to train you to give the service

Answer: B. Schedule collaboratively

Collaborative scheduling of students to receive services is both your responsibility and that of the service provider. Scheduling together allows for both your convenience and that of the service provider. It also will provide you with an opportunity to make sure the student does not miss important information.

(Skill 5.8) (Average)

114. The best way to ensure the success of educational interventions is to:

   A. Give regular education teachers the primary responsibility of teaching special needs students in regular classrooms

   B. Give special education teachers the primary responsibility of teaching special needs students in special education classrooms

   C. Promote cooperative teaching efforts between general and special educators

   D. Have support personnel assume the primary responsibility for the education of special needs students

Answer: C. Promote cooperative teaching efforts between general and special educators

Both types of teachers can learn from each other. Special education and regular education teachers should demonstrate the attitude that the exceptional student is a student of both teachers, not a special education student who only goes into a general education classroom at certain times.

(Skill 5.8) (Average)

115. A serious hindrance to successful mainstreaming is:

   A. Lack of adapted materials

   B. Lack of funding

   C. Lack of communication among teachers

   D. Lack of support from administration

Answer: C. Lack of communication among teachers

All four choices are hindrances, but lack of communication and consultation between the service providers is the most serious.

(Skill 5.8) (Easy)

116. Jane is a third grader. Mrs. Smith, her teacher, noted that Jane was having difficulty with math and reading assignments. The results from recent diagnostic tests showed a strong sight vocabulary, strength in computational skills, but a weakness in comprehending what she read. This weakness was apparent in mathematical word problems as well. The multidisciplinary team recommended placement in a special education resource room for learning disabilities two periods each school day. For the remainder of the school day, her placement will be:

   A. In the regular classroom

   B. At a special school

   C. In a self-contained classroom

   D. In a resource room for mental retardation

Answer: A. In the regular classroom

An emphasis on instructional remediation and individualized instruction in problem areas as well as a focus on mainstreaming is characteristic of the resource room, a special room inside the school environment where the child goes to be taught by a teacher who is certified in the area of disability. It is hoped that the accommodations and services provided in the resource room will help her to catch up and perform with her peers in the regular classroom.

(Skill 5.9) (Easy)

117. **All of the following are essential components of effective parent-teacher conferences EXCEPT:**

   A. Collecting samples of student work, records of behavior, and other relevant information

   B. Beginning the conference with positive comments about the student

   C. Using informal small talk to put the parents at ease

   D. Preparing a list of questions or concerns you wish to address

Answer: C. Using informal small talk to put the parents at ease

While you do want to begin the conference by putting the parents at ease and by taking the time to establish a comfortable mood, you should not waste time with unnecessary small talk. Begin your discussion with positive comments about the student, and be polite and professional. By collecting relevant data and a list of questions or concerns you wish to address, you will be better prepared to keep the conference focused and positive.

(Skill 5.9) (Average)

118. **Parent contact should first begin when:**

   A. You are informed the child will be your student

   B. The student fails a test

   C. The student exceeds others on a task

   D. An IEP meeting is scheduled and you have had no previous replies to letters

Answer: A. You are informed the child will be your student

Student and parent contact should begin as a getting to know you piece, which allows you to begin on a nonjudgmental platform. It is counterproductive to wait until there is a problem. If you can establish a cordial, team spirit relationship with the parents in the beginning, it will be easier to solve problems when they arise. It also helps the parent to see you as a professional that is willing to work with them.

(Skill 5.9) (Average)

119. **You should prepare for a parent-teacher conference by:**

   A. Memorizing student progress/grades

   B. Anticipating questions

   C. Scheduling the meetings during your lunch time

   D. Planning a tour of the school

Answer: B. Anticipating questions

It pays to anticipate parent questions. It makes you more likely to be able to answer them. It is also possible that anticipating them may be a way for you to plan what to speak to the parent about.

(Skill 5.9) (Rigorous)

120. Lotzie is not labeled as needing special education services, but he appears to be unable to function at his grade level both academically and socially. He is in 9th grade, but reads picture books and consistently displays immature behavior that can be misinterpreted. You have already observed these behaviors. What should be done first?

   A. Establish a rapport with the parents

   B. Write a CSE referral

   C. Plan and discuss possible interventions with the teacher

   D. Address the class about acceptance

Answer: A. Establish a rapport with the parents

When a student enters 9th grade in a poor placement such as this, it is not unusual for the parents to have been opposed to special education. The best way to help the student is to establish a rapport with the parents. You need to find out why he has not been referred, and if possible, help them see why their child would benefit from special education services.

CPSIA information can be obtained at www.ICGtesting.com
Printed in the USA
LVOW02165530041 3
331639LV00003B/48/P